sharing plates

Acknowledgments

After finishing this, my second cookbook, I find myself sitting in front of my computer, taking stock of what I have just completed. This is the first time that I have had a chance to really think about the book from a distance, and I feel humbled and honoured to have been given the opportunity to share my passion for food. There are many people who I would like to give a 'verbal cuddle' by way of acknowledging their efforts and hard work.

Huge thanks to all of the Murdoch team, especially Juliet Rogers and Kay Scarlett for having enough faith in me to allow me to do it again; Jacqueline Blanchard and Zoë Harpham for being wonderfully patient and supportive; Vivien Valk for her beautiful design; Margot Braddon for her 'fresh eyes'; and, of course, the talented Mr Alan Benson who has been an absolute inspiration and pleasure to work with.

I would also like to thank my passionate and enthusiastic team at Danks Street Depot who have been a great support; in particular Penny Williams, Tim Allan, Symone Murphy, Tom Olesen and Kate Shearer. This team is one of the reasons I find myself enthralled by the restaurant industry—it is not just a world of food, but a chance to work with people who inspire me, offer support and share their passions. This book is as much a result of their hard work as anyone's.

I'd also like to take this opportunity to thank anyone who produces food with passion and integrity, anyone who cooks food with enthusiasm and care, and anyone who enjoys food and the pleasures of the table.

And, of course, thanks to Melanie and Charlie for being my little family.

sharing plates

Jared Ingersoll

A table for all seasons

MURDOCH BOOKS

Contents

Introduction

I opened Danks Street Depot with my beautiful wife and partner, Melanie Starr, in 2002 for one simple reason—the love of good food and the pleasure of sharing it. The idea of *Sharing Plates* is all about celebrating the pleasures of the table: it is about food, it is about drink and, most importantly, it is about coming together. This book is the direct result of the second Thursday of every month at Danks Street Depot, which has become famous as our 'Bar Food Night', which is the night where we take time to acknowledge the importance of sharing plates. Bar Food Night is in turn a direct result of every meal I have cooked for friends and family! I have rarely cooked a meal at home where I have individually plated separate meals for my guests—after all, why would you? That's why you have restaurants! When you dine at my table, you are a welcome guest, an equal, and we will share our meals, swap stories, laugh and enjoy!

Jared

Spring menu
for a shared table

Drinks

12   Plum tequini
12   Poached pear martini
14   Jared's bloody mary
15   Rhubarb mojito

Nibbles

16   Potted prawns with frisée and chive salad
19   Onion rings with parmesan mayo

Share plates

20   Barbecued cuttlefish and crispy pancetta with a chilli zucchini
      and a tahini dressing
22   Asian green salad with nam jhim
26   Crab and harissa soup with zucchini fritters
29   Ham hocks steamed in hay
30   Bresaola with peas and marjoram
32   Roasted whole leatherjacket with romesco sauce
35   Carrot and coriander seed salad
36   Buffalo mozzarella with broad beans and a chopped lemon sauce

Desserts

38   Apricot gratin with buffalo yoghurt and raspberry coulis
39   Fig biscotti with mascarpone cream and dessert wine
42   Lemon and mint granita
43   Gulab jamin

Plum tequini

for one

I owe my barman, Chris, a great deal for showing me this drink. Prior to working with him, the last time I had drunk tequila was in Mexico and I woke up with my head sticking out of my tent and the door zipped down to my neck! Needless to say I was feeling a little ill (not to mention sunburned and insect-bitten) when I woke, and I was quite adamant that I would never again touch tequila. Fast forward about 8 or so years and there I was enjoying this cocktail with its robust plum flavour over an enticing tequila base. As it turns out, the great flavour combination of plum and tequila was enough to convince me I could drink tequila.

1 very ripe blood plum, stone removed
45 ml (1½ fl oz) tequila
1 teaspoon shaved palm sugar (jaggery)
ice

In a cocktail shaker, place your plum, tequila and the palm sugar and muddle well. Add plenty of ice and shake vigorously. Double strain into a chilled cocktail glass. Once you have poured off as much of the drink as you can, take a teaspoon of the pulp from the strainer and carefully place into the bottom of your glass.

Poached pear martini

for one

I love this martini because it shows how easy it is to make a great cocktail. It is a common mistake to think that a cocktail requires multiple flavours and complicated techniques, but this one reminds me that a simple understanding of ingredients can produce a truly remarkable drink. When Tom Olesen first started work as my barman, I invited him to taste some of the fruit syrups that we use in the kitchen. He had one sip of the pear syrup and ran off to the bar, applied some bar magic and the pear martini was born. You may want to experiment with different fruits and spirits, which is easy as long as you understand the basic principles. The beurre bosc pear imparts a distinct texture and not-too-sweet pear flavour to the poaching liquid, which means that the martini has a slight pear mouth-feel. I like to use Wyborowa vodka as it has a sweet flavour and velvety texture that I believe enhances the pear texture. Now you know this, you can change the ingredients and make up your own mind. The other great thing about this drink is that even though it does require a little preparation (preferably the day before), it is easy to make so it is ideal for large groups. The syrup makes enough for 12 drinks.

For the pear syrup

500 ml (17 fl oz/2 cups) water
400 g (14 oz/1¾ cups) sugar
1 lemon, zest cut into pieces, juiced
2 vanilla beans
4 ripe beurre bosc pears

Put the water, sugar, 2 or 3 pieces of the lemon zest and all of the juice from the lemon into a saucepan. Carefully scrape out all the vanilla seeds and add them, along with the vanilla bean, to the saucepan.

Peel the pears, then cut in half and remove the cores. Thinly slice the pears and place into the water. Place the saucepan onto a high heat and bring to the boil. Allow to boil for only 5 minutes, then remove from the heat and allow to cool in the fridge. When completely cold, strain the syrup through a coarse sieve, gently pushing on the pear to remove as much of the juice as you can, but taking care not to push through too much of the pear pulp. What you should end up with is a delicious pear and vanilla syrup that will keep in the fridge for about 1 month.

For the martini

45 ml (1½ fl oz) vodka
20 ml (½ fl oz) pear syrup
ice

Shake the vodka and pear syrup together over plenty of ice in a cocktail shaker, then single strain into a chilled martini glass to serve.

Jared's bloody mary

for one

This is a drink that holds a very special place in my heart—working the Sunday brunch shift at the Bayswater Brasserie in Sydney was always punctuated by a knee-wobblingly powerful bloody mary. Nowadays, I prefer to have a little less kick (vodka) than I did during those good old days, but I still love a well-flavoured and well-balanced bloody mary. The only way I vary from the classic recipe is that I prefer to blend my own tomato juice and I make a celeriac salt to season the drink—you'll end up with enough of each of these for several cocktails.

For the tomato juice

1 kg (2 lb 4 oz) overripe tomatoes
a splash of red wine vinegar
a pinch of salt
a splash of extra virgin olive oil

When you have perfectly overripe tomatoes, make your own juice; if not, you can get away with a really good-quality tomato juice. When you go to make your own tomato juice, remove any seeds from the tomatoes, and place the flesh into a blender with the red wine vinegar, salt and oil. Blend until well puréed, then strain through a sieve to remove any solids. Your juice will keep for 2–3 days in the fridge, but it will need to be shaken well before use.

For the celeriac salt

1 head of celeriac
salt

Peel and grate the celeriac and combine on a tray with approximately an equal volume of salt (for example, 1 cup salt to 1 cup grated celeriac), then mix well. Leave this to dry completely. This can be achieved by leaving the mixture in the sun (out of the wind) or by setting your oven to the lowest possible temperature and then placing the mixture into the oven and stirring from time to time to ensure that it dries out properly. When your mixture is completely dry and brittle, pound into a powder with your mortar and pestle and store in an airtight container. This will keep for months.

For the bloody mary

ice
½ teaspoon celeriac salt
4 grinds of black pepper
a dash of Tabasco sauce
3 dashes of worcestershire sauce
15 ml (½ fl oz) dry sherry
45 ml (1½ fl oz) vodka
200 ml (7 fl oz) tomato juice, chilled
1 stalk of celery, preferably the pale celery heart with a little of the leaf left on for good looks
a splash of lemon juice

Fill a highball glass with plenty of ice and start adding your ingredients. Begin with the seasonings, then the sauces, then the alcohol and, finally, the tomato juice. Stir really well with your celery stalk. Taste for seasoning, and add a little of the lemon juice to the top of your drink. Sip, stir and chomp away.

Rhubarb mojito

for one

2 large or 3 small stalks of rhubarb
2 tablespoons sugar
4 leaves of mint
¼ lime
ice
60 ml (2 fl oz/¼ cup) white rum, such as
    añejo blanco
splash of soda water, optional

Thinly slice the rhubarb and sprinkle it with the sugar and let it sit overnight if you wish, or you can just go straight on to making your drink. Put the rhubarb and mint in a cocktail shaker. Squeeze in the lime juice and add the crushed lime wedge. Fill with ice to the top. Pour in the rum and shake really, really well. Pour into a tall glass—if you need to top it up, add a splash of soda water to the cocktail shaker and wash any remaining cocktail into the glass. Serve straight away.

When I was a kid, we had this great big rhubarb plant growing outside the kitchen window. One of my favourite things to do was to chop off a stalk and sit down with a little dish of sugar, dip the rhubarb into the sugar and chomp away.

This drink is a play on the traditional lime-based mojito—I like the way the extremely sour rhubarb is mixed with sugar and mint. To get the most vivid colour from your rhubarb, sugar it down the day before (there is no difference in flavour). The rum you use is up to you; my preference is for Havana añejo blanco as it has a sweet fruitiness to it that works well with the rhubarb.

Potted prawns with frisée and chive salad

for eight to ten as a nibble

This is something you can make up to a week in advance and have ready to simply drop on the table when everyone is ready. It's a bit of an old-school classic—I first ate this a few years ago in a café, in the English seaside city of Brighton, with a mug of tea for lunch. Though it is very rich, it is a delicious way to start a meal. I have changed the basic flavours of the classic recipe slightly to make it more aromatic, which helps when eating a big serve of butter.

1 kg (2 lb 4 oz) very fresh school prawns
   (shrimp)
300 g (10½ oz) butter
2 star anise
6 bay leaves
4 green cardamom pods, cracked open
a generous pinch of cracked white pepper
a generous pinch of salt

Blanch the prawns in water on a rolling boil for about 2 minutes, then plunge into iced water. Drain, then start to peel, putting the peeled prawns into a bowl. This may seem a little daunting as school prawns are tiny and fiddly, but there is a trick to it—most of the shell is soft enough to eat, so all you need to remove are the harder parts of the prawn (that is, the head, legs and tail). And don't forget to daydream while doing this.

While you are peeling, put the butter and all of the other ingredients in a saucepan over a very low heat to allow the flavours to infuse. After about 30 minutes (which should be long enough to peel the prawns), strain off the solids from the butter and put the butter in the fridge to cool a little.

When the butter is cool (but not set; if the butter sets, melt it again), pour the butter over the prawns and gently stir. Taste the prawns and check for seasoning— you want them to be well seasoned, almost too salty, as this is going to be served cold. Pour the prawns into ramekins or one dish that is just big enough to fit all of the prawns snugly, then pour over all of the butter. You want the prawns to be covered by the butter, so poke down any rogue bits—you may even have to melt a little more butter. Refrigerate for at least 3 hours.

Remove from the fridge about 40 minutes before you want to serve, which should be just long enough to take off the chill.

For the frisée and chive salad

100 g (3½ oz) French shallots, finely chopped
a pinch of salt
a pinch of sugar
a few grinds of black pepper
80 ml (2½ fl oz/⅓ cup) white vinegar
3 heads of frisée (curly endive)
200 ml (7 fl oz) extra virgin olive oil
1 bunch of chives, finely snipped

Put the shallots in a small bowl and season with the salt, sugar, pepper and vinegar. Leave to sit for about 20 minutes to allow the shallots to pickle slightly. Meanwhile, carefully remove the bitter tough outside dark green leaves of the frisée and reserve the golden to pale green inner leaves. Whisk the oil into the shallot mixture and check the seasoning. Add your leaves and chives and toss well.

For serving

toast
a few wedges of lime, optional

To assemble, place the dish of prawns on a platter (or individual plates) alongside the salad, and serve with some toast and perhaps some lime wedges. Provide a couple of bread knives to make it easier to eat.

Onion rings with parmesan mayo

for four to six as a nibble

This recipe uses one of my favourite batter recipes. Although it is normally used in Indian cuisine and may seem a little out of context here, it works really well. The parmesan mayo needs to be made from oil infused with parmesan rinds, which you should have because you were so influenced by my first book that you started saving your parmesan rinds and will now enjoy the fruits of your labour! If you don't have home-made parmesan oil, you can either buy it from a gourmet food store, or you can make a plain mayonnaise instead.

For the chickpea flour batter

220 g (7¾ oz/2 cups) besan (chickpea flour)
175 g (6 oz/1 cup) rice flour
a pinch of asafoetida
a pinch of chilli powder
a pinch of salt
400 ml (14 fl oz) iced water in which 1 teaspoon bicarbonate of soda (baking soda) has been dissolved

Combine your dry ingredients in a large bowl, then make a well in the centre. Using a whisk, start to slowly add your iced water and gradually combine all of your ingredients into a batter that has the consistency of pouring cream. Keep in the fridge until you are ready to use it—the batter can be made the day before but don't try to keep it any longer than that.

For the parmesan mayo

juice of ½ lemon
2 egg yolks
a touch of dijon mustard
200 ml (7 fl oz) parmesan-infused oil
salt and ground black pepper

You can make this mayonnaise in a bowl with a whisk, but it is easier in a food processor. Whisk or blend the lemon juice, egg yolks and mustard together. Slowly and carefully add your oil, making sure that it emulsifies before adding more. When you have finished adding your oil, season to taste with salt and pepper.

For the onion rings

2 large onions
a touch of plain (all-purpose) flour for coating the onion rings
oil, for deep-frying

Peel your onions, then cut into discs about 1 cm (½ in) thick. Break the discs up into rings (the mystery of how this dish got its name is now revealed) and toss the rings in a little flour. Put the onion rings in the batter, shaking off any excess flour as you do so.

When it comes to perfectly deep-frying the onion rings, read the introduction 'How to cook the perfect fries' (page 138). Take a large saucepan and fill it no more than one-third full of oil. Bring your oil up to 175°C (350°F), then carefully lower in a small batch of the onion rings and cook for 3–4 minutes, or until golden and crispy. Be careful not to overcook them as they really are at their best when crunchy on the outside and fluffy in the middle. Repeat with the rest.

For serving

salt
wedges of lemon or lime

When your onion rings are golden and crispy, drain thoroughly on paper towel, then season with a little salt. Put onto a plate next to a dish of your mayonnaise and a few wedges of lemon or lime.

Barbecued cuttlefish and crispy pancetta with a chilli zucchini and a tahini dressing

for four to share

If you have never eaten cuttlefish before, then make a point of trying it. At first glance you may think that cuttlefish looks just like squid, and it is in fact very similar to squid—if you have trouble finding cuttlefish you can substitute squid. My preference for cuttlefish stems from the fact that I prefer its 'crunchy' texture and I find its meat tastes cleaner and sweeter than that of squid.

This is a dish that I have been making on and off for years—I love the combination of the sweet crunch of cuttlefish with the earthy flavours of the zucchini and tahini, enhanced by tangy, salty pancetta.

For the chilli zucchini dressing

4 zucchini (courgettes)
2 cloves of garlic, crushed
2 large red chillies, seeded and finely chopped
185 ml (6 fl oz/¾ cup) olive oil
salt and ground black pepper

Finely dice the zucchini—I find the easiest way to do this is to slice it lengthways on a mandolin first, then cut the zucchini into strips and, finally, into small dice. This is a little fiddly but the result is well worth it.

In a bowl, combine your zucchini, garlic and chilli, then heat a little of your oil in a large frying pan over medium–high heat and fry some of the zucchini. You want to cook your zucchini until it is a beautiful golden colour, which will give an amazing sweet flavour to your dressing; when you are cooking the zucchini you don't want to have too much in the pan at a time, so it may pay to cook it in batches unless you have a very large frying pan. When you have a nice light brown colour on the zucchini, transfer it to a clean bowl, wipe out the pan and repeat the process until all the zucchini is cooked. Season with salt and ground black pepper.

For the crispy pancetta

8 pieces of pancetta

You want to start by making sure that you buy 'flat pancetta' that is sliced to order. What I have found is that pre-sliced pancetta can dry out and may taste a little dull—there should be more to the flavour of pancetta than just that of salty pork.

Preheat your oven to 180°C (350°F/Gas 4). Lay out the pancetta on a baking tray lined with baking paper and bake for about 10 minutes, or until crispy. Carefully lift your pancetta onto paper towel to drain.

Barbecued cuttlefish and crispy pancetta with a chilli zucchini and a tahini dressing

For the tahini dressing

2½ tablespoons tahini
1½ tablespoons lemon juice
salt and ground black pepper
water
sugar, optional

Put the tahini in a bowl, then whisk in the lemon juice, salt and pepper. As soon as you start to incorporate liquid into tahini, it will thicken—adjust the consistency with water until it resembles pouring cream. I really like the bitter flavour of tahini, but if you prefer you can sweeten with sugar.

For the cuttlefish

16 even-sized cuttlefish
vegetable oil
salt and ground black pepper

If you don't mind cleaning fish, then I would recommend that you buy whole cuttlefish and clean them when you get home as you'll get a better result. However, if you prefer, you can ask your fish supplier to clean it for you.

To clean the cuttlefish, take the body in one hand and the legs in the other and use a gentle pulling motion to remove the legs and innards. Use your fingers to pull out the remaining guts. Take the body of the cuttlefish in your hands and use your thumb to push out the bone and then, using a dry tea towel (dish towel) to help you get a grip of the skin, gently peel away the skin. Rinse the cuttlefish under cold running water, then pat dry. Repeat the process with the rest of the cuttlefish.

Take your cleaned cuttlefish and, with a sharp knife, very carefully make shallow slashes across the cuttlefish, then give it a quarter turn and cut across the first cuts so that the cuttlefish has tiny little squares cut into it. Place all of your cuttlefish into a bowl and drizzle with a little oil and season really well. Place the cuttlefish onto a hot barbecue or grill plate and cook for about 1½ minutes on one side and 30–40 seconds on the other.

For serving

a few leaves of mint
about 100 ml (3½ fl oz) verjuice

Put the cooked cuttlefish in a clean bowl with your chilli zucchini dressing, mint leaves and the verjuice and combine really well. Arrange the cuttlefish on a platter and drizzle with the tahini dressing, then arrange the pieces of pancetta over the top.

Asian green salad with nam jhim

for eight to share or four for a meal

A few years ago, I was working on a function to showcase the quality of fresh produce from around the Sydney Basin region. The function organizer and I were knocking around some ideas about how to best utilize the produce we had available. He said, 'Just make a salad of some sort from the Asian greens'. This was a novel idea as Asian greens are by no means a 'salad green' and there would have to be care taken in preparing them, plus the term 'Asian' covers a whole lot of ground. My head chef, Penny, and I got together and discussed what an 'Asian salad' constitutes; this is a great way to work towards a new dish as we both had a pretty good knowledge of different aspects of Asian cooking. We agreed that the salad had to be big in flavour, have a good touch of heat from chilli and have a slightly pickled character to it. We decided to use a Vietnamese-style dressing called nam jhim, which is a great little number to know as it is both delicious and versatile—I use this dressing with everything from roasted pork to boiled prawns (shrimp).

The trick to this dish, as with any of my recipes, is to use the best produce of the day. You can substitute any vegetable here for another—what makes the salad special is that you make a powerful nam jhim dressing to enhance wonderful vegetables that have been cooked to perfection. You can adjust the heat of the dressing by altering the number of chillies and whether you include the seeds or not (the more seeds, the hotter the dressing).

Asian green salad with nam jhim
pictured page 24

For the nam jhim

2–3 bird's eye chillies
3 French shallots
1 clove of garlic
roots from 1 bunch of coriander (cilantro) (you'll
 need the leaves for the salad)
85 g (3 oz) palm sugar (jaggery), shaved
juice of 3 limes, about 80 ml (2½ fl oz/⅓ cup)
80 ml (2½ fl oz/⅓ cup) fish sauce

To make the nam jhim, you need either a very large mortar and pestle or a small food processor. A mortar and pestle will give the best results because pounding all of your ingredients into a fine paste helps to release the flavour, giving a nicer texture to the dressing. Cut your chillies in half—whether or not you remove the seeds is up to you.

Place the chillies, shallots, garlic and coriander roots in the mortar or food processor and pound or blend really well—be careful that the chilli does not splash out and get you in the eyes. When your solid ingredients become a paste, add the palm sugar and pound or process until dissolved, then, using a stirring motion, add the lime juice and fish sauce. Your dressing should be very intense but have a good balance of heat (chilli), salt (fish sauce), sweet (palm sugar) and sour (lime juice). After you taste your dressing you may need to adjust the seasoning accordingly until it is balanced.

For the toasted rice

100 g (3½ oz/½ cup) jasmine rice

Add the rice to a clean, dry, cold frying pan and toast over a gentle heat until the rice is a pale straw colour. Allow it to cool, then grind with your mortar and pestle until you have a fine powder.

For the vegetables

½ Chinese cabbage (wong bok)
1 bunch of bok choy (pak choy)
1 bunch of choy sum (Chinese flowering cabbage)
1 bunch of gai larn (Chinese broccoli)
a pinch of salt

To prepare your vegetables, you first need to make a decision about what size to cut them; this will depend a lot on their natural size. What you are aiming for is all the chopped vegetables to be roughly the same size, but the size you pick is completely up to you. When in doubt, 3–4 cm (1¼–1½ in) pieces usually work well. It's worthwhile keeping in mind that if your pieces are too large the dish will be tricky to serve.

Cook the vegetables briefly in plenty of well-seasoned boiling water, then plunge into iced water and, finally, drain off all the excess water (too much water on your greens means you will end up diluting your dressing). The cooking time depends on your vegetable: the cabbage needs no more than 30 seconds and the vegetables with thick stalks can take 2–4 minutes, but their leaves need less time. Start tasting your vegetables after they have been plunged into boiling water and remove them when you judge them to be perfect.

For serving

1 bunch of mint, leaves picked
the leaves from the bunch of coriander (cilantro)
 left from the nam jhim
a small knob of ginger (young ginger if
 available), peeled and cut into thin strips

To serve, simply ensure your vegetables are dry, and combine them in a large bowl with your mint and coriander leaves, ginger strips and add most of your dressing (reserve a little to finish the salad). Toss well and taste, adding more dressing or nam jhim ingredients as required; for example, if you think it needs to taste sourer, add an extra squeeze of lime. When you are completely happy with the flavour, mound your salad onto a platter, splash over a little more dressing and sprinkle with the toasted rice.

Crab and harissa soup with zucchini fritters

for eight to share

For the soup

- 3 whole live blue swimmer crabs
- 1 teaspoon cumin seeds
- 1 teaspoon caraway seeds
- 1 teaspoon coriander seeds
- ½ teaspoon fenugreek seeds
- 80 g (2¾ oz/⅓ cup firmly packed) soft brown sugar
- a pinch of chilli flakes
- salt and ground black pepper
- 150 ml (5 fl oz) vegetable oil
- 3 red capsicums (peppers), seeded and chopped
- 2 cloves of garlic, crushed
- 4 ripe tomatoes, chopped
- 1 red onion, chopped
- 1.5 litres (52 fl oz/6 cups) fish stock
- 1 bunch of coriander (cilantro)
- a few sprigs of mint
- a few sprigs of flat-leaf (Italian) parsley

Preheat your oven to 180°C (350°F/Gas 4). I think the most humane way to kill a crab is to use a heavy knife and drive the tip of the knife into the top of the head, just above and in between the eyes, then cut all the way through in one swift movement; this will kill the crab instantly. To clean the crab, take hold of the body of one crab with one hand and then take hold of the head of the crab with your other hand. Lifting sideways, lift the head away from the body and detach. Inside you will see the gills (they look like little fingers) on either side of the head, and some brown meat. Keep the brown meat but make sure that you remove all of the gills. Use a heavy chopping knife to cut the crab into quarters and place into a large bowl. Repeat the process with the other crabs.

Toast the cumin, caraway, coriander and fenugreek seeds in a dry frying pan until fragrant. Grind with a mortar and pestle. Sprinkle the spices over the crab along with the sugar, chilli flakes, salt and pepper.

Heat a deep roasting tin in the oven. When the tin is nice and hot, add the oil and then the crab and spices. Mix everything together really well, then cook in the oven for about 20 minutes. Every so often bring the crab out and use a heavy mallet or a rolling pin to smash the crabs up. Once the crabs have started to take on a spicy, roasted flavour, add the capsicum, garlic, tomato and onion, mix about, then continue to cook for about 1 hour, making sure that every now and then you bring the tin out, give everything a really good stir and smash any unbroken pieces of crab. You will know that the crab and vegetables have finished roasting when you have an amazing roasted aroma, and you are starting to get just a little colour, but you don't want to brown anything too much. When you are ready, lift the roasting tin out of the oven and place on top of your stove over a low heat.

Add the fish stock to the tin and let everything gently simmer for 10–15 minutes, then taste and adjust the seasoning accordingly. Transfer to a large saucepan or pot, add your herbs and, using a stick blender, blend the soup as best you can. You won't be able to blend through all of the crab shells—but give it a really good go as you want to get as much flavour from the shells as possible. When everything is well blended you will need to pass the mixture through a mouli, using a fine plate to collect all the little shards of shell. Take time to squeeze out as much of the soup as you possibly can; only stop using the mouli when you are left with a dry crumbly mixture on top.

Once you have passed your soup through the mouli, set it to one side and start making the fritters.

For the zucchini fritters

    4 large zucchini (courgettes)
    salt and ground black pepper
    2 eggs, beaten
    140 g (5 oz/heaped 1 cup) plain (all-purpose)
        flour
    a pinch of salt
    a tiny pinch of chilli flakes
    vegetable oil, for frying

Grate the zucchini, then season with a little salt and allow to drain for about 30 minutes. Squeeze out as much of the liquid as you can from the zucchini, then place into a bowl with the egg, flour, salt and chilli. Mix together into a batter. Heat a large frying pan with about 2 cm (3/4 in) of vegetable oil over medium–high heat and add dollops of the zucchini mixture, a tablespoon at a time. When golden on one side, flip them over and cook the other side. When they are ready, lift out of the pan and place onto paper towel to drain. Repeat with the rest of the zucchini batter.

For serving

While preparing the fritters, reheat your soup without letting it boil. Serve the soup in a large tureen with a pile of the fritters on the side.

I love cooking this recipe. I like the effort that you have to put in, the crushing of the crabs, the roasting and the smell in the kitchen as it is being prepared. You do need a mouli to press the soup, as any other method is way too labour intensive, and just straining through a sieve alone will not give you all of the flavour. You may look at this recipe and ask, 'Why don't you just remove the meat from the crab and make a stock from what's left?' Well, just try it my way and I'm sure you will agree that this method will give amazing results because you are using every single ounce of flavour the crab has to offer.

Harissa is a Tunisian hot sauce made from chillies, garlic and spices. This soup is based on the flavours of harissa.

Ham hocks steamed in hay

for six to share

I stumbled across this technique of cooking meat quite by accident—in fact I have to admit that I was a little dubious about the results, but nothing compared to the reaction I got from my suppliers when I tried to source a good supply of hay. I made a few phone calls to people who I knew owned farms to ask where I could source some hay, and the best advice I got was to try a pet food supplier that specialized in food for horses. As it turned out, there was one just around the corner from the café. I called them on the phone. 'I need some good, clean hay to cook with and it needs to be organic because I don't want to be eating some weird chemicals.' The girl I spoke to didn't even hesitate before replying, 'Sure. No problem, we have a pile that arrived yesterday'. I have to admit that I was quite amused firstly that there was a demand for organic hay and secondly that she didn't seem to think it unusual that I wanted to cook with hay. As it turns out, a majority of the grazing lands in Australia are organic simply because they haven't been sprayed with chemicals yet; those that are regularly sprayed tend to be heavily farmed areas. Also, the family of the girl I spoke to used to cook in hay. At this point I would like to offer one really important piece of advice—when buying anything from a store with great big letters across the front saying 'Pet Food' it is best not to wear a chef's uniform. It simply sends the wrong message to any customers who may be driving by, as I discovered when I returned to the café in time to receive a phone call from a concerned regular.

That aside, the reason that you cook in hay is that it gives you a wonderful gentle heat in which to cook your meat, almost like steaming it in beautiful lush pastures. During the cooking process the kitchen will fill with the most intoxicating grassy aroma but, interestingly enough, the flavour itself is delicate and subtle. I have allowed about one ham hock between two people.

a bundle of organic hay
3 whole smoked ham hocks

Preheat your oven to 200°C (400°F/Gas 6). You need a very large ovenproof pot that can fit into your oven. Start by preparing the hay—to do this, fill your sink with cold water and give the hay a really good soak, then rinse. Do this a couple of times, refilling the sink with clean water each time, being sure to get rid of any dirt. Now pack the hay into the bottom of your pot. Push the ham hocks down into the hay bed and then cover with more hay; firmly pack down as much hay as you can. When you have as much hay in the pot as possible, start pouring fresh cold water into the pot until the pot is about three-quarters filled with water. Place the pot on top of your stove over a high heat and cook until you start to see a good head of steam. Add the lid and put in the oven for about 2 hours.

To test if the ham is cooked, simply push a carving fork into the hay and skewer the ham hock—the meat should be soft and allow the fork to easily penetrate all the way to the bone. Lift out the ham hocks and rinse them to remove any bits of hay.

I like to serve the ham hocks alongside some boiled potatoes seasoned with butter, salt and pepper, and some piquant mustard or pickles.

Bresaola with peas and marjoram

for eight to share

Bresaola is an air-dried beef that is usually made from silverside. The raw meat is cured in a mixture of red wine, herbs (such as rosemary and bay) and spices (such as pepper and cloves). After it has been preserved in the brine it is then allowed to air dry, which gives the beef its distinct flavour and texture. You can buy bresaola from Italian delicatessens; you should always make sure that it is being sliced as you order. This will not only ensure that it is soft and full of flavour, but also that it is being sliced as thinly as possible. Bresaola works really well with the sweetness of the peas and marjoram in this dish, but you can substitute the bresaola for prosciutto if you prefer.

300 g (10½ oz) fresh green peas, podded
a few sprigs of marjoram
salt and ground black pepper
125 ml (4 fl oz/½ cup) extra virgin olive oil
about 16 thin slices of bresaola
a small piece of parmesan cheese, grated

Take your peas and blanch them in salted water for 2–3 minutes, then drain and immerse straight away into iced water to stop the cooking process. Drain again. Place the peas into a large mortar, remove the leaves of the marjoram and add to the peas, then crush everything together with some salt, pepper and about half of the olive oil. You don't want a purée—just crush until you have a coarse mash.

Arrange your bresaola on a plate, then drizzle with the remaining olive oil and season with a little salt and pepper. Place a mound of the peas on your beef, then finish with some freshly grated parmesan.

Roasted whole leatherjacket with romesco sauce

for four to share

For the romesco sauce

6 large ripe tomatoes

1 bulb of garlic

60 ml (2 fl oz/¼ cup) olive oil for frying, plus extra, for drizzling

2 ancho chillies (a large dried chilli with a smoky flavour) or other large, dried chillies

500 ml (17 fl oz/2 cups) hot water

1 large stale croissant, cut into thick slices

50 g (1¾ oz/⅓ cup) blanched almonds

50 g (1¾ oz/⅓ cup) hazelnuts, lightly toasted and skins removed

1 teaspoon paprika

60 ml (2 fl oz/¼ cup) red wine vinegar

salt and ground black pepper

250 ml (9 fl oz/1 cup) extra virgin olive oil

You need to prepare a couple of the ingredients before you start to make the sauce base. Preheat your oven to 250°C (500°F/Gas 9). Take the tomatoes and cut them in half and place on a non-stick roasting tray, cut side down. Slice the bulb of garlic crossways, about two-thirds up the head, and place the larger half, cut side up, next to the tomatoes (reserve the remaining garlic). Drizzle with a little of the olive oil and place in the oven until the skin on the tomatoes starts to blister and the garlic gets nice and brown. You don't want any burnt bits but you do want a really good colour—this can take up to 30 minutes.

While the tomatoes and garlic are cooking, prepare the rest of the ingredients. Place a dry frying pan on a high heat, put the ancho chillies in the pan, press down with a spatula and scorch until you see a little wisp of smoke (about 10 seconds), then flip them over and scorch the other side. Remove from the pan and place into a bowl with the hot water and allow to soak for about 15 minutes, or until they soften. Remove the stem and any seeds, then set to one side.

Wipe out your frying pan and, while it is still hot, add the extra olive oil and gently fry the pieces of croissant for about 10 seconds on each side until golden brown, then drain on paper towel.

Remove the remaining raw garlic from its skin and place into a food processor with the soaked chillies, nuts, paprika and the fried croissant. Blend really well, taking time to scrape down the side from time to time. By now your tomatoes should be ready, so take them out of the oven and, when cool enough to handle, pinch off the tomato skins and add the flesh and any cooking juices to the food processor. Take the garlic and squeeze out the roasted garlic flesh into the food processor bowl. Blend everything again with the vinegar and a good amount of salt and pepper. While the processor is running, very slowly add the extra virgin olive oil in a steady stream until everything is incorporated. Transfer the sauce to a bowl and taste, adding more salt, pepper and vinegar as required.

This is now ready to use or you can store it in the fridge for up to 2 weeks.

For the roasted whole leatherjacket

4 x 300–400 g (10½–14 oz) whole
leatherjackets or other whole firm, white fish
300 ml (10½ fl oz) chicken or fish stock
a splash of dry white wine
vegetable oil, for frying
salt and ground black pepper

Preheat your oven to 200°C (400°F/Gas 6). Have your fishmonger clean the fish by removing the head (leatherjacket is one of the few fish I remove the head from before cooking) and cutting away the fins. If you are using another type of fish, leave the head on.

Start by pouring your stock and just a little white wine into a saucepan; when it has just come to the boil, add 500 g (1 lb 2 oz/2 cups) of your romesco sauce and give a really good stir. Place a lid on your saucepan and then turn the heat right down and let it barely simmer for about 30 minutes. The nuts and croissant in the romesco sauce will start to swell up and will give the sauce a nice consistency.

To cook the fish, either do it in batches in an ovenproof frying pan or roast them all together in one roasting tin. Start by heating the pan or roasting tin on the stove with a little oil; when the dish is very hot, season your fish and carefully add to your pan or tin. Cook on one side for about 5 minutes, then turn over and cook the other side for about 2 minutes until it is sealed. Tip off any excess oil and pour in your hot romesco sauce, then transfer the pan or tin to the oven and cook for about 8 minutes, or until the fish gives under your finger when you push it.

For serving

2 tablespoons sesame seeds, toasted
a few sprigs of coriander (cilantro)
a few wedges of lime

Scatter the fish with toasted sesame seeds and coriander. Take the fish straight to the table and serve with wedges of lime. It goes well with a crisp salad.

Having romesco sauce on hand all the time will make your life so much better. The sauce will sit really well in your fridge for a couple of weeks, but will also freeze well. It does involve a little time to prepare it correctly, and it contains a couple of unusual ingredients, so I strongly recommend making a big batch like I have done here and storing away what you don't use (this recipe leaves you with about 500 g (1 lb 2 oz/2 cups) leftover sauce after cooking the fish). Romesco sauce does taste a lot better if it is made the day before. You can serve your romesco sauce with most grilled or roasted meats or, if you are like me, you will smear it on some fresh bread as a snack. Another thing about this romesco sauce recipe is that its techniques are very similar to that for a mole (a Mexican classic), which can be quite involved and complicated—romesco sauce is a great stepping stone before tackling a mole.

Leatherjacket is a fish that often gets overlooked as it has a strong and distinct taste, but it works really well in this recipe. If you can't get hold of leatherjacket, then pretty much any fish that you want to roast whole will do.

Carrot and coriander seed salad

for four to six to share

This is an incredibly easy salad to prepare. All the ingredients are there to enhance the natural flavour of the carrot, so you need to have the best possible carrots: juicy, sweet and flavoursome. The type, size and shape of the carrot are secondary to the flavour, so make sure you taste a little piece of carrot before going any further.

500 g (1 lb 2 oz) beautiful, tasty carrots
a pinch of salt
a pinch of sugar
2½ tablespoons coriander seeds, lightly toasted, then roughly crushed
1 small stalk of rosemary, leaves only
1–2 large red chillies, seeded and thinly sliced lengthways
60 ml (2 fl oz/¼ cup) verjuice or mild white wine vinegar
80 ml (2½ fl oz/⅓ cup) extra virgin olive oil
plenty of salt and ground black pepper

Start by preparing your carrots, which for this recipe means doing as little as possible to them. If you are using baby carrots, perhaps just gently scrape off the skin and leave them whole; if you are using great big carrots, then they may need to be peeled and cut into pieces—the decision is up to you.

Bring a saucepan of water to a rolling boil and add a good pinch of salt and the same amount of sugar, then add the carrots and cook them for the briefest time possible—they must still be wonderfully sweet and crunchy. When they are cooked to your liking, lift them out of the water and plunge into iced water to stop the cooking process. As soon as they are cool, drain, then put them in a large bowl.

In a separate bowl, add the coriander seeds, rosemary, chilli, verjuice and olive oil and gently whisk to combine the flavours. Add some salt and ground black pepper and taste again. Pour the dressing over the carrots and toss them together really well, then let them sit for at least an hour. Taste them again before serving to see if you need to alter the seasoning, as the chilli will have started to come out and the verjuice will have penetrated the carrots.

Buffalo mozzarella with broad beans and a chopped lemon sauce

for four to share

You must use fresh mozzarella for this recipe, and if you are lucky enough to get hold of some that has been imported from Italy, then grab it. I know I am always going on about the importance of using fresh local produce, but there are exceptions and fresh mozzarella from Italy is definitely one of those—it just cannot be beaten. But a word of caution: mozzarella will deteriorate very quickly and, in Australia, the guys who import this amazing cheese are always on a race against time (and customs). Fresh mozzarella should feel nice and firm; old mozzarella will start to go a little flowery around the edges and absorb a little too much of the water in which it is stored.

The lemon sauce in the recipe is slightly bitter and should be used sparingly. Although this recipe makes a lot more sauce than you need, this is something you'll be glad to have in your fridge—it works well with grilled meats and fish, or even splashed over some spaghetti with loads of freshly grated parmesan and freshly chopped parsley for a super quick pasta dish. This sauce will keep for at least a month in the fridge in an airtight container.

Buffalo mozzarella with broad beans and a chopped lemon sauce

For the lemon sauce

4 lemons
a pinch of salt
2 cloves of garlic, crushed through
    a garlic press
a pinch of chilli flakes
6 anchovy fillets, coarsely chopped
300 ml (10½ fl oz) extra virgin olive oil
    (a rich, peppery one will be best here)

Take each whole lemon and cut into quarters. Remove the seeds. Place the lemon quarters on your chopping board, skin side down. Remove the flesh of the lemon and put to one side, but leave the skin and pith intact. Slice the quarters of lemon skin lengthways into very thin strips. Place your strips of lemon skin into a saucepan and cover with cold water and a pinch of salt. Bring the water to the boil, then drain. Tip your lemon strips onto a tea towel (dish towel) to absorb any excess water—this process will remove some of the bitterness from the lemon skin.

Now return your lemon strips to the saucepan with the crushed garlic, chilli flakes, anchovies and extra virgin olive oil. Place your pan onto a very gentle heat and slowly bring to a simmer; as soon as it simmers, remove from the heat. Now take the lemon flesh and chop coarsely. Add the lemon flesh to your saucepan and bring back to a very gentle simmer, then turn off the heat and leave to cool to room temperature. You don't want to cook the sauce for very long at all, just long enough to ensure that the lemon and garlic soften and the flavours all come together.

For the broad beans

about 1 kg (1 lb 2 oz) fresh broad (fava) beans or
    350 g (12 oz/2 cups) podded broad beans
a pinch of salt

If you are using fresh broad beans in their pods, you need to remove the beans from their pods. Once you have done that (or if you are using podded broad beans), you will see that you have a pale green bean; if you remove the skin of the bean, there is a bright green bean under the pale green skin. When the beans are young and tender at the beginning of their season you can eat the bean skin and all. As the season progresses and the beans become larger, you will notice that the skin will become tougher and taste slightly bitter and will need to be removed. To do this, simply bring a saucepan of salted water to a rapid boil. Drop your beans into the water for no more than a moment, remove the beans from the boiling water and plunge them straight into iced water to stop the cooking process. Drain the beans and, using a pinching action, squeeze the beans out of their skins.

For serving

4 large balls of fresh mozzarella cheese
½ bunch of basil
a drizzle of extra virgin olive oil
salt and ground black pepper

To serve this salad, take the mozzarella and tear it into chunks and arrange it onto your plate, then scatter over some of the broad beans and torn basil leaves. Now drizzle over some of your lemon sauce. Drizzle with a little more extra virgin olive oil, then season with salt and plenty of pepper.

Apricot gratin with buffalo yoghurt and raspberry coulis

for eight

If you can't find buffalo yoghurt, then any plain yoghurt will do the trick—the appeal of the buffalo yoghurt is that it has a delicious, almost dry finish to it, and even though it has a fairly high fat content its flavour is clean and light. This is a great dessert for those who don't want to overload on sugar but appreciate a fruity finish to their meal.

For the crumble

60 g (2¼ oz/⅔ cup) walnut halves
80 g (2¾ oz/½ cup) pistachio nuts
80 g (2¾ oz/½ cup) blanched almonds
80 g (2¾ oz) unsalted butter
60 g (2¼ oz/½ cup) plain (all-purpose) flour
60 g (2¼ oz/⅓ cup) soft brown sugar
a tiny pinch of salt

Put the nuts in a food processor and pulse until they are coarsely chopped, then add the butter and pulse once or twice to combine. Scoop this mixture into a bowl, then add the flour, sugar and salt. Using your fingertips, rub everything together until the mixture feels like damp sand. Place the crumble mixture in the fridge until you are ready to use it.

For the coulis

300 g (10½ oz/2½ cups) frozen raspberries
140 g (5 oz/heaped 1 cup) icing (confectioners')
  sugar
lemon juice, to taste

Put the raspberries and icing sugar in a small saucepan over low heat; when the sugar is dissolved and the mixture is just about to simmer, put in a food processor and blend thoroughly. Taste and add lemon juice accordingly—you want just a hint of lemon juice to help cut through the sweetness of the sugar. When completely blended, push through a fine sieve.

For serving

8 small ripe apricots or 4–6 larger ones (or
  235 g/8½ oz drained tinned apricots)
a small tub of buffalo yoghurt

If you are using fresh apricots, bring a saucepan of water to the boil and blanch the apricots for just long enough to see the skins starting to split, then lift them straight out with a slotted spoon and plunge into iced water. When they are completely cool, take out of the water and slip off the skins. Using a small knife, cut in half around the stone, then make a twisting motion to separate the two halves, using the tip of a knife to dig out the stone.

Place the apricot halves, cut side up, onto a baking tray, take your crumble mix out of the fridge and pack the crumble into each apricot half to create a mound. Place the apricots as far as possible from the heat source under a preheated medium–low grill (broiler) for about 10 minutes, or until the crumble mixture turns golden. Remove from the grill, pour your coulis onto a platter, arrange the apricots on the puddle of coulis, then place spoonfuls of yoghurt next to the fruit.

Fig biscotti with mascarpone cream and dessert wine

pictured page 40

for eight

I am one of those people who absolutely must finish a meal with something sweet, regardless of how full I am. The beauty of this dessert is that it is very simple to prepare and serve, and it suits those times when everyone may be quite full from the meal but still wants something sweet to nibble. The other great thing is that any leftover biscotti keeps very well in an airtight container.

For the biscotti

500 g (1 lb 2 oz/4 cups) plain (all-purpose) flour
a pinch of salt
½ teaspoon baking powder
165 g (5¾ oz) unsalted butter, at room temperature
200 g (7 oz/scant 1 cup) caster (superfine) sugar
2 eggs
165 g (5¾ oz/1 cup) dried figs, chopped
1 tablespoon honey
1 lemon, zest finely grated
1 orange, zest finely grated
1 extra egg, beaten for egg wash
80 g (2¾ oz/⅓ cup) caster (superfine) sugar, extra

Preheat your oven to 170°C (325°F/Gas 3). In a bowl, combine the flour, salt and baking powder. In a separate large bowl, cream the butter and sugar by beating with a wooden spoon until it becomes light and fluffy, then beat in the eggs until combined. Add the figs, honey and citrus zest, then beat well. Add the flour and form into a dough with your hands.

Divide the dough in half and, working on a floured surface, shape it into two logs each about 20 cm (8 in) long. Place them onto a piece of greased baking paper and then lift the paper onto a baking tray. Brush with the beaten egg and sprinkle with the extra sugar.

Bake the logs for about 20 minutes, or until golden. Remove from the oven and cool on a wire rack. When cool, place them onto a chopping board, then slice on an angle into 1 cm (½ in) thick pieces—

you should get about 20 slices from each log. Lay the slices onto a greased baking tray and bake for about 5 minutes, then turn them over and bake for another 5–6 minutes. The biscotti must be golden and completely dry and crispy—if they are still soft they will not store as well. Cool on a wire rack.

For the mascarpone cream

300 g (10½ oz/1⅓ cups) mascarpone cheese
150 ml (5 fl oz) pouring (whipping) cream
120 g (4¼ oz/heaped ½ cup) sugar
a touch of mixed grated lemon and lime zest
a splash of lemon juice

Beat everything together with a wooden spoon until light and creamy.

For serving

a bottle of dessert wine

Place the mascarpone cream in a small bowl, then make a well in the middle and pour in some of your favourite dessert wine. Place the bowl on a platter surrounded by the biscotti and take to the table with a serving spoon, the bottle of wine and some little plates, for everyone to help themselves. The idea is to take a biscotti, drizzle over a little extra wine, spoon on some of the mascarpone and enjoy.

Lemon and mint granita

for eight

pictured page 41

This is an extremely simple frozen dessert and one that is delicious and refreshing. The other great thing is that it takes very little effort to experiment with other flavours. How about adding a little gin? Perhaps some lemoncello? Or what about infusing the water with something other than mint?

1 litre (35 fl oz/4 cups) water
320 g (11¼ oz/1½ cups) sugar
1 bunch of mint
200 ml (7 fl oz) lemon juice
shredded mint, extra

Put the water and sugar together in a saucepan and bring to a boil. Once it has boiled, add the bunch of mint and lemon juice and allow to cool completely. Strain the liquid through a fine sieve to remove all of the solids, then taste the syrup. When food is frozen it is slightly harder for your taste buds to pick up on some of the flavours, which means that when you taste the liquid at this stage you want it to be slightly too sweet and too lemony. When you are happy with the flavour of the syrup, pour into a container and place in the freezer for at least 24 hours. When you remove the granita from the freezer it will be a solid block of ice, so what you want to do now is use a fork to start to scrape and 'fluff up' the surface of the granita. Serve in chilled glasses, garnished with a little extra mint.

Gulab jamin
for ten

This is a classic Indian dessert that almost every Indian restaurant serves. For those of you who don't mind a little sugar in your diet, then this is the recipe for you! I used to work in an Indian restaurant in New Zealand and I had the bad habit of making up reasons for the morning chef in charge of the preparation to leave the kitchen, just so I could sneak into the cool room and have a quick feast on gulab jamin. Sure, the flavour is nicer when they have been heated but nothing tastes better than a sneaky dessert! I am sure that the chef, who was newly arrived from Delhi, is still telling stories back in India about how bad the telephone system is in New Zealand and how every time he was told there was a phone call for him, the line was dead by the time he got there. To do this recipe justice, you do need to venture out and buy yourself some ghee, which is essentially clarified butter: it will give the dessert its distinctive taste.

For the syrup

600 ml (21 fl oz) water
600 g (1 lb 5 oz/2¾ cups) sugar
2 teaspoons rosewater
a good pinch of saffron threads

Put all the ingredients in a saucepan and bring to the boil; continue to boil for 2–3 minutes before removing from the heat and allowing to cool—it doesn't need to cool completely.

For the batter

500 g (1 lb 2 oz/5 cups) milk powder
4 tablespoons melted ghee
about 125 ml (4 fl oz/½ cup) cold water
1.25 kg (2 lb 12 oz) ghee, extra, for cooking

Use your hands to mix the milk powder and melted ghee together really well, then start adding the cold water a tablespoon at a time. Mix thoroughly each time before adding more water and continue until all the water is used. Continue to knead the mixture until a smooth dough forms. Divide the dough into 15 equal pieces and roll each piece between the palms of your hands until you have formed a ball, about 3 cm (1¼ in) in diameter.

While you are doing this, place the ghee for cooking into a large deep saucepan that will fit all 15 balls in one batch, side by side, and sprinkle them with a few drops of water. Place the pan over a medium heat and heat until the ghee melts and the water starts to splatter. Add the balls of dough and continue to cook over a medium heat for about 5 minutes, turning the balls from time to time until they are deep golden colour all over. Carefully remove from the ghee and place onto a paper towel for a brief moment, then drop into the syrup that you prepared earlier.

You want the gulab jamin to soak in the syrup for at least 10 minutes but you can very easily place the finished dessert into the fridge for a day or two, reheating as needed. Just remember that when you serve the gulab jamin they are supposed to be eaten as they are, literally swimming in a pool of the syrup. Every now and then, when I feel like being fancy, I splash over a shot of warmed Cointreau and set fire to it for effect.

Summer menu
for a shared table

Drinks

Nibbles

Share plates

Desserts

Classic bellini

for one

This drink was originally created at Harry's Bar in Venice. It is rumoured that the bar used to employ one person who worked full time doing nothing more than squeezing the peaches by hand in order to extract their juice. Almost any bar that you go to will be able to serve you some sort of version of the bellini, but when we sell it at Danks Street Depot we believe that it must be prepared as closely to the original recipe as possible, and for that reason it is only available for the 3 months of the year when white peaches are at their absolute best. This is a lovely brunch drink as it is really not too boozy at all. It should always be made with a nice dry Prosecco (Italian sparkling wine).

There is a variation of the bellini that is great to serve in the winter months, a mimosa, which is made in much the same way but instead of peach juice you use a mixture of freshly squeezed orange and tangerine juice.

For the white peach juice

white peaches
sugar, optional

We do vary (slightly) from the original recipe by using a food processor to help us make the peach juice. Blanch your peaches in plenty of boiling water until the skins have started to split. Place them immediately into a bowl of iced water. When cool, remove the skin from the peaches and cut in half to remove the stone. Place the peaches into a food processor and blend really well until completely liquidized, then pass through a sieve. Taste your juice as it may need a little sweetening; if so, just add a little sugar. This juice is best on the day; the next day the flavour will still be passable but you may notice a bit of discolouration.

For serving

100 ml (3½ fl oz) freshly squeezed white peach juice
200 ml (7 fl oz) Prosecco
1 teaspoon butterscotch schnapps, optional

Chill all of your ingredients thoroughly. Pour the peach juice into a chilled champagne glass, then top up with the Prosecco. A nice touch (that has nothing to do with the original recipe) is to add about 1 teaspoon of butterscotch schnapps to the drink—it is something that you won't really be able to taste, however it will give your drink a little more depth.

Cucumber and mint Pimms cup

for about four

In my last book I gave a recipe for cured cucumbers that I said were absolutely delicious served with Pimms punch but, as so many of you have quite rightly pointed out, I provided no recipe for the mouth-watering glass pitcher of Pimms punch shown in the photograph. Well, here it is. You can, of course, add fruit to your Pimms but I find the combination of cucumber and mint to be simply perfect.

ice
1 cucumber, sliced into strips on
    a mandolin
1 bunch of mint
200 ml (7 fl oz) Pimms No.1
300 ml (10½ fl oz) lemonade (lemon-lime soda)
200 ml (7 fl oz) ginger ale

In a large glass pitcher, add some ice, cucumber and mint, then add more ice, cucumber and mint, layering it throughout the pitcher (this layering does nothing other than make sure it looks pretty). Now add your Pimms, then top up with the lemonade and ginger ale. Gently stir.

Mint julep
for one

A mint julep is supposed to be sipped out of a silver 'julep' cup while listening to the slow southern drawl of fellow drinkers watching the Kentucky Derby. This may not always be possible but I do believe a mint julep is the perfect way in which to enjoy good bourbon.

I might just take a moment to tell you about professional barmen. A good barman is the perfect combination of chemist and artist and has an obsessive compulsive disorder. To test this theory, just get a room full of barmen together and ask them how you should make a julep. Some will argue the benefits of making a mint syrup, others how and when to bruise the mint, how and when to add the mint, what sort of mint, how much mint, how to present the mint and how much mint aroma should be inhaled while sipping. And that is before you even get to adding the other ingredients to the glass! I do have to admit that when Chris, my barman, makes me a julep I get very excited and I have never tasted one to equal his, so maybe there is something in all of this after all.

ice
8 leaves of mint
2 teaspoons caster (superfine) sugar
60 ml (2 fl oz/¼ cup) bourbon

Half-fill a lowball tumbler (or your silver julep cup) with ice, then place half of the mint leaves in the palm of your hand and give them a good slap—this will slightly bruise them and let them release their aroma. Add this to the glass with half the sugar and half the bourbon and give this a really good stir. Now add more ice, repeat the process with the remaining mint, add the remaining sugar and bourbon and again stir really well. Now there is one trick to enjoying a julep that I will swear by: your straw needs to be just over the lip of the glass so that as you sip you get a noseful of the mint.

The Waterloo

for one

Before opening up a bar in the Sydney suburb of Waterloo, I thought that I should have a drink named after the area. After all, the name Waterloo is pretty famous after Napoleon Bonaparte's final battle in 1815, so I was sure there would be a drink in its honour. I poured over books, looked on the internet, asked barmen all over town and I became very excited—I could find no cocktail called 'The Waterloo'. I started experimenting—it had to have the feel of a classic cocktail but not be boring, and I wanted to make a drink that I would enjoy, which for me means something very alcoholic that you can sit on for a while and casually sip. After many attempts I found this. I hope you enjoy it. I prefer Martell VSOP cognac, which goes incredibly well with the orange and raisin flavours.

1 cm (½ in) thick slice of orange, unpeeled
2 raisins or currants
1 cm (½ in) piece of vanilla bean
¼ teaspoon grated palm sugar
1 dash of Angostura bitters
2 splashes of soda water
ice
45 ml (1½ fl oz) cognac

You need to get a little physical making this drink so don't make it in a delicate glass; a good thick 'old-fashioned' glass or cocktail shaker is best. Start by putting in the orange, raisins, vanilla, palm sugar, bitters and a tiny splash of soda water. Now, using a rolling pin or a wooden spoon, start crushing all the ingredients together, making sure to pulp the orange flesh really well—this should take you a couple of moments. Then add plenty of ice and your cognac, stir really well and then finish off with just a little splash of soda water.

Salmon mousse with a baby herb salad and melba toast

for eight as a nibble

It is funny how food trends come and go. I remember when I first started cooking, it was almost unheard of to have a menu that did not include salmon mousse in some form or another. Over my time I cannot count the number of salmon mousse recipes I have come across; in fact I used to see how many different recipes I could collect. So after all my collecting and much trial and error I can say with complete honesty that a good salmon mousse relies solely on good-quality salmon. I have also found that if the salmon has been too heavily brined or smoked at too high a temperature and too quickly that it will affect the oil content in the fish, which will affect the flavour and the final texture of the mousse.

I like to serve the mousse with a salad of baby herbs. There is a guy living just outside Sydney who has started to produce 'baby herbs' or 'micro herbs'. At first I thought that it was a little gimmicky, but after experimenting with different types of herbs and meeting the guy and talking about how the herbs are produced, I have completely changed my mind. They may be a little hard for you to get hold of, but if you can they are really worth the bother. If you can't get them, then simply use normal herbs and take care to choose small leaves so that you have the effect of a fine, pretty salad.

The melba toasts are delicate and wonderful; when you make them, you will be surprised that you can get anything so good out of a stock-standard piece of pre-sliced white sandwich bread. A single slice of bread will make eight little toasts, which will be enough for a snack for one person.

Salmon mousse with a baby herb salad and melba toast

For the salmon mousse

300 g (10½ oz) cold-smoked piece of salmon
a pinch of cayenne pepper
salt
220 g (7¾ oz/1 cup) thick (double/heavy)
    cream (or as much as you want)

You will get the best results if everything that you use to make the mousse is very cold, so what I normally do is put the food processor bowl along with another large bowl and any utensils in the freezer for a while to chill everything.

Start by blending the smoked salmon in a food processor to a fine paste, using a rubber spatula to scrape around the inside of the bowl to ensure that it is evenly blended. While it is blending, add the cayenne pepper and salt.

Transfer the salmon purée to your chilled bowl and, using a rubber spatula, start adding the cream a little at a time, being sure to combine all of the cream before you add any more. The trick to a good mousse is to only mix it as much as you absolutely need to—if you blend the salmon too much it will start to warm up and this will change the final texture, and also if you beat the cream too much it can split and become grainy and have a nasty fatty taste. So just remember to only work it as much as you absolutely have to, which means you may not need quite as much as the recipe states.

For the herb salad

about 2 handfuls of mixed baby herbs
a drizzle of olive oil
a squeeze of lemon juice
salt and ground black pepper

Place the herbs into a small bowl and very lightly dress with the olive oil and lemon juice. Season with salt and pepper.

For the melba toasts

8 slices of white bread

Preheat your oven to 170°C (325°F/Gas 3). Lightly toast one side of the bread under the grill (broiler). Allow to cool, then cut off the crust while trying to keep your piece of bread as square as possible. Using a large sharp knife, carefully split the bread through the middle so that you end up with two pieces of bread with one side toasted and the other side being soft bread. Cut each piece into four triangles. Now comes the fun part. You want to 'rub' the soft bread off the toasted bread—you can do this by placing one of the little triangles on your chopping board, toasted side up, then press the palm of your hand down on the bread quite firmly and start to make little circles. After a couple of moments you should end up with a wafer-thin slice of toasted bread; don't panic if there is still a little of the bread on the toast. Once you have rubbed all of your bread, place the triangles onto a baking tray, toasted side up, and then into the oven for 5–6 minutes until they curl up slightly and go a crispy golden brown. Once they have cooled they will be very fragile so be careful how you handle them, as nothing is as annoying as breaking all of your toasts before you get to show them off.

For serving

wedges of lemon

I like to simply put down one nice big blob of mousse with a mound of the herb salad next to it and a couple of wedges of lemon to be squeezed over the mousse as desired. Next to this I put a few plates, a couple of knives and a pile of melba toasts.

Scallop and avocado salsa with little flat bread crackers

as a dip for ten or lunch for five

This salsa should have a good chilli kick, which is not so good for the kids, but my 3-year-old son is more than happy just munching away on the dense and crunchy crackers. This recipe will make about 40 little flatbread crackers, but you can easily make larger crackers and then break them into pieces—my preference for little crackers is solely based on the fact that they look cute!

For the crackers

500 g (1 lb 2 oz/4 cups) plain (all-purpose) flour
a good pinch of sugar
a good pinch of salt
50 g (1¾ oz) butter, at room temperature
375 ml (13 fl oz/1½ cups) warm water
your choice of seeds, spices or chopped herbs

In a large bowl, combine the flour, sugar and salt and make a well in the centre. Add the butter to the warm water and, when the butter is completely melted, add it to the flour. Mix in the liquid and then knead the dough until it is nice and smooth. Wrap the dough in a piece of plastic wrap and refrigerate for at least 1 hour.

Preheat your oven to 190°C (375°F/Gas 5). Line a baking tray with baking paper and lightly grease the paper. The easiest way to shape your crackers is by using a pasta machine on the thickest setting. If you don't have one you can get just as good results using a rolling pin; it will just take a little longer.

Place your dough onto a lightly floured surface and use your hands to roll into a 40 cm (16 in) long log, then take a sharp knife and cut into 40 even 1 cm (½ in) discs. Dampen a tea towel (dish towel) and drape this over any dough you are not working with so it doesn't dry out. Take one of the discs and briefly roll it between your palms to form a rough sausage shape, then either roll it with a floured rolling pin or put it through the pasta machine. The end result should be about twice the size of an ice block (popsicle) stick. Place onto your baking tray (you may have to do this in batches) and lightly spray with a little water. Sprinkle with your choice of topping, such as seeds, spices or chopped herbs.

Bake for 8–12 minutes and, when brown and crisp, transfer to a wire rack to cool completely. When cool, test a cracker. If they are not completely crisp and dry, they can be returned to the oven; if your crackers are not crisp enough at this stage you will find that they will start to go quite soft if you try to store them for any length of time. They should last for a couple of weeks if stored in an airtight container.

For the salsa

24 large, fresh cleaned scallops, roe removed, finely diced
2 fresh habanero or bird's eye chillies, seeded and finely chopped
juice of 2 limes
1 teaspoon sesame oil
2 tablespoons sesame seeds, toasted
a drizzle of olive oil
salt, to taste
3 ripe reed avocados, diced the same size as the scallops

For the best results, make this just before you want to serve. Prepare all of your ingredients and place into a large bowl—except for the avocado; this should be done last minute to avoid discolouring. Use a spatula or a wooden spoon to gently combine the mixture, trying not to crush the avocado. Serve with the crackers.

Marlin poke

for eight to share

Poke, pronounced 'poh-kay', is the Hawaiian word for 'cut pieces' and is quite simply a fish salad that can be eaten raw or, in this case, seared very briefly. I have experimented with different fish, such as scallops, swordfish, mackerel and tuna, but have found that marlin, cooked for the briefest of moments, will give you amazing results. Marlin is very similar to swordfish in its structure, but I think more closely resembles kingfish in flavour. The marlin that I typically get is striped marlin and I prefer the piece to come from a fish that is 6–8 kg (13 lb 8 oz–18 lb) in size. The best place to buy marlin, as with any fish, is from your local fishmarket, as the less handling it receives between the catch and your plate the better. Marlin flesh can become damaged more easily than other fish if not handled correctly. Marlin should smell tangy but sweet and the flesh should feel firm and moist. When I buy it, I like to cut off a small sliver and taste it raw—this is the best way to ensure the quality of your product.

600 g (1 lb 5 oz) marlin fillet (preferably
    mid-cut)
2 tomatoes, peeled, seeded and coarsely chopped
250 g (9 oz) fresh seaweed, chopped, or
    5 g (1/8 oz) dried wakame
1 teaspoon grated fresh ginger
1 handful of chopped spring onion (scallion)
3 French shallots, chopped
100 g (3 1/2 oz/3/4 cup) crushed macadamia nuts
1 tablespoon sesame oil
2 tablespoons soy sauce
salt and ground black pepper
vegetable oil
a sprinkling of sesame seeds, toasted
1 head of cos (romaine) or iceberg lettuce
wedges of lime
soy sauce, for serving

Dice your marlin into 1 cm (1/2 in) cubes and place into a large bowl. When you are ready to cook your fish, add to the bowl the tomatoes, seaweed, ginger, spring onion, shallots, macadamias, sesame oil, soy sauce and salt and pepper, and taste a small piece of marlin to check for seasoning. What you will end up with is a bowl of raw fish salad—you can in fact serve it as it is or you can proceed to the next stage and briefly cook the mixture.

When it comes to cooking the poke, you want to do this as fast as possible, literally searing the outside of the fish and leaving the middle slightly raw. The easiest way to achieve this is in a very hot wok with vegetable oil, cooking in batches to ensure that everything is cooked evenly. When you have cooked all of the fish, place it on a platter with a scattering of sesame seeds. Next to it place some lettuce leaves, lime wedges and a little dish of soy sauce. Invite your guests to place the fish onto the lettuce and eat with their hands.

Baked vongole
for four to share

pictured page 58

Vongole is the name given to baby clams, and the beauty of vongole is that they are tiny sweet explosions of flavour. Just remember that when you buy vongole you should ask whether or not they have been 'purged' to remove the gritty sand. If not, it is an easy thing to do yourself—just rinse, then soak your vongole in plenty of cold water for no less than 8 hours and no longer than 24 in a cool, dark place or even in the fridge. This will give them enough time to open up and flush fresh water through themselves, which will remove any grit and sand. The cooking method used here is easily adapted to other shellfish, such as clams, pipis and mussels.

The bruschetta makes a great snack. I allow 1–2 slices of bread per person.

For the bruschetta

4–8 thick slices of sourdough bread
olive oil, for drizzling
salt and ground black pepper
a couple of cloves of garlic

It is easier if you cook your bruschetta before the vongole—simply drizzle the bread with a little olive oil and season before placing on a baking tray and then into a preheated 180°C (350°F/Gas 4) oven. When the bread is nice and golden, rub each piece with a little of the raw garlic. Keep warm while cooking the vongole.

For the vongole

40 vongole
2 tomatoes, peeled, halved and seeded
2 cloves of garlic
55 ml (1³⁄₄ fl oz) extra virgin olive oil
125 ml (4 fl oz/½ cup) dry white wine
1 bunch of thyme
1 bay leaf
a good grinding of black pepper
a pinch of salt

Rinse off your purged vongole. You want to wrap the vongole in a double layer of foil, so lay out a sheet that you feel will be big enough to take the vongole and then lay out another sheet on top. Tip on the vongole and all the other ingredients, taking care not to let the liquids spill out. Now wrap up the vongole into a foil parcel; when you are wrapping, make sure that you leave enough room for the clams to open up comfortably.

Place a dry frying pan onto a high heat and, when it is good and hot, add the vongole parcel and push down a little to ensure the parcel is fitting snugly on the bottom of the pan. When you start to see steam coming out of the parcel, continue to cook for about another 5 minutes, shaking the pan from time to time to ensure even cooking (as if you were making popcorn). Remove the pan from the heat and transfer the whole parcel, unopened, to a platter. Serve immediately by placing the platter in the middle of your group. Use a pair of scissors to cut open the foil parcel—take care though as the foil will cool very quickly and may not feel hot to touch, but inside a good head of steam is just waiting to burst out. Serve with the bruschetta.

Kingfish swimming
for ten to share as a starter

This dish can only be done with success when you have beautiful young ginger and fresh young coconuts. And, as the name suggests, it should always be served in a dish 'swimming' in the mild dressing made from the coconut water—you simply will not get the same results by using coconut milk or cream. I normally buy a whole fillet of Hiramasa kingfish that weighs 900 g–1.1 kg (2 lb–2 lb 7 oz), which is ideal for about 10 people for a starter; if you want to serve it as a main meal, then you should double the recipe. As you will be serving the kingfish raw, take care to purchase the best and freshest fish you can find.

When it comes to making the dressing, the puritan will insist that the ingredients need to be left whole, then pounded with a mortar and pestle to give the best texture and flavour. The theory is that simply chopping or blending will not give you the same intensity of flavour. However, if you're in a hurry, chop or blend away.

For the dressing

- 3 bird's eye chillies, seeds and stems removed
- 2 French shallots
- 1 clove of garlic, peeled
- 1 coriander (cilantro) root
- 100 g (3½ oz) shaved palm sugar (jaggery)
- 80 ml (2½ fl oz/⅓ cup) lime juice
- 80 ml (2½ fl oz/⅓ cup) fish sauce
- 1 fresh young coconut full of water, (make sure you give it a shake to hear the water sloshing about inside)

If you are using a mortar and pestle, I will warn you and say that it will be a bit of a workout; if you feel like taking it easy you can use a food processor. Whichever way you do it, you really need to take the time to make sure the chillies, French shallots, garlic and coriander root are completely puréed before adding the other ingredients.

Place the chillies, French shallots, garlic and coriander root into a large mortar or a food processor and smash or process until you have a fine paste. Add the palm sugar and pound or blend a little more to dissolve, then add your lime juice and fish sauce. Taste the dressing; it should be very powerful but well balanced—you want it to be hot (chilli), sweet (palm sugar), salty (fish sauce) and tart (lime juice), so add more of whatever your taste buds want. When you are happy with the flavour, pour the dressing into a bowl.

Young coconuts are relatively soft and should pose no problems to get into them. Use the heel of a large chopping knife and carefully start to hack a circle into the top of the coconut until you are able to lift off the top. Stir the dressing while you slowly pour in the coconut water until you have a nice soft dressing—remember that you want the kingfish to be 'swimming' in the dressing so you don't want the flavour to be too strong. Now use a large spoon to scoop out the soft silky flesh of the coconut and place onto a chopping board, and then slice into very thin strips.

For the kingfish

1 whole fillet of kingfish, 900 g–1.1 kg
(2 lb–2 lb 7 oz)

To skin the kingfish fillet, place the kingfish, skin side down and lengthways along your chopping board. Position a sharp knife just up from the tail of the fillet and make a small cut across the fillet down to the skin, but not through the skin. Position the fillet so that you can take a firm grasp of the little cut piece of flesh at the tail in one hand, then slide the knife under the fillet but above the skin of the fish. The next stage should be done in as clean a motion as you can. Angle the blade of your knife slightly towards the skin and apply just a little downward pressure as you slice along the fish using a slow sawing motion—the skin should come completely away in one piece but any little pieces of skin left behind can be removed later. You can do the above or you can buy some slices of kingfish sashimi from your local sushi restaurant, but I reckon this takes out a lot of the fun of this dish.

For serving

4 cm (1½ in) long piece of fresh ginger
1 large red chilli
2 avocados
a few leaves of coriander (cilantro) and mint

I like being able to serve the kingfish as individual little mouthfuls that are soaked in the dressing, so I usually either place each piece of fish on a skewer or serve with a little glass of toothpicks or short skewers nearby.

Take your ginger and peel it, then cut into nice thin strips. Take the chilli and cut in half lengthways, scrape out the seeds and cut into thin strips. Cut your avocados in half and remove the stones. Now take your kingfish and cut into thin slices across the fillet.

To serve, use a platter or plate with a high lip and lay out the pieces of kingfish on the platter. Use a teaspoon to scoop out chunks of the avocado, then place a chunk over each piece of kingfish. Top this with the strips of ginger and chilli, then scatter over the leaves of coriander and mint before pouring the dressing over each little pile. Serve immediately.

Smoked eel with potato and bacon salad

for eight to share

When I was a kid we used to fish for eels by first leaving a piece of meat outside for about 3 days until it got really stinky. We'd then tie the meat to a piece of string and, when it got dark, we'd head down to the river armed with a torch and a broom handle that had a great big nail taped to one end. We would then lower the rancid meat into the water and wait ... as soon as we felt a tug on the meat we'd turn the torch on and try to spear the eel. It is with sad nostalgia that I write this recipe because I remember the fun I used to have by the river near where I grew up in New Zealand—the rafting, fishing and good old-fashioned fun. However, recently I took my son back to my childhood home, only to discover that all the places I used to visit as a kid are now fenced off with signs warning that due to pollution anyone entering does so at their own risk, and other signs saying that eating anything from the river will cause health problems. Not only is this kind of thing a tragedy for the environment, but what saddens me the most is that it makes it even harder for people to enjoy catching and cooking food for themselves.

1 whole smoked eel (these are usually between
875 g–1 kg/1 lb 15 oz–2 lb 4 oz)
1 bunch of watercress, picked and washed
1 small piece of fresh horseradish or a couple of
spoonfuls of pickled horseradish
8 pieces of smoked bacon
16 small cooked cocktail potatoes, cut in half
lemon juice, to taste
250 ml (9 fl oz/1 cup) extra virgin olive oil
½ bunch of flat-leaf (Italian) parsley, leaves
coarsely chopped
salt and ground black pepper

Locate the gills of the eel, which are just at the base of either side of the head. Position a sharp knife at this point, then cut down to the spine. Now make a smooth sawing motion down the length of the fish to remove the top fillet. Flip the eel over and hang the head over the edge of the board to make the eel lie nice and flat. Repeat the same process to remove the other fillet, then discard the frame and the head. Place your fillets, skin side down, on your chopping board. Starting at the tail end, slide your knife under the flesh and above the skin. Take a firm grip on the skin and, using a smooth motion, slide your knife along the board to remove the skin. You can snip off any little pieces of skin that you have missed.

This is a warm salad, which means that you want to cook and serve it straight away, so you will need to make sure that you have all of your ingredients ready to go. Put the watercress in a large bowl and have ready a fine grater to grate the horseradish to finish off the salad. To begin, cut the bacon into pieces that are roughly the same size as the eel, then put them in a large frying pan over a medium heat and cook until they start to go crispy. Turn and cook the other side. When the bacon is cooked, lift it out of the pan and put to one side, but be sure not to discard any of the bacon fat—you want to use this as part of the dressing.

Add the potatoes to the pan and move them about just enough to warm them, then turn off the heat and gently add the pieces of eel just long enough to warm them. Squeeze in your lemon juice, add the olive oil and chopped parsley and season really well. Now tip everything into the bowl with the watercress and, using a wooden spoon or your hands, carefully fold all of the ingredients together. Grate on as much of the horseradish as you want and mix again. Arrange your salad on a platter, top with your pieces of bacon and then finish with a little more grated horseradish.

Brined and roasted quails with agresto sauce

for six to share

I can easily eat two quails at a sitting so use this as a guide when thinking about how many to cook. I find that when it comes to presenting this dish I simply put all of the quails in the middle of the table and have everyone dig in. It is a good idea to provide finger bowls and napkins because the best way to eat a quail is with your fingers.

In the *Danks Street Depot* cookbook I talked about how to salt a duck before roasting and the advantages of doing so. Here is another fantastic cooking technique—brining. I have found that to get wonderful flavour and an amazing finish to roasted quail (this will also work with spatchcock and chicken) it is best to brine them. Brining is a term used for when you submerge food in liquid, commonly salted water, and allow the food to cure slightly. You can of course use this brining stage to introduce other flavours but the most important ingredient is the salt. Brining allows the salt water to penetrate through the skin and into the muscle, which will give you a moist, flavoursome bird.

There are a couple of things that you need to pay attention to when brining. Make sure that your brine is chilled before adding your meat; if the brine is too hot it may start to cook your meat and you also run the risk of promoting bacterial growth as the meat and brine cool down together. Always keep the brining meat in the fridge. Take care when adding more salt to the meat during the cooking process as it should be seasoned well enough from the brine.

You can add whatever flavours you want to the brine—when you are experimenting with flavours just remember that you get the best results when balancing out the saltiness with sweetness. It's very important to never use acidic ingredients as the acids will start to cook and discolour the meat.

A whole chicken can sit in the brine for 8–12 hours, a spatchcock 4–5 hours and quail about 3–4 hours. Don't leave the meat in the brine for longer than this, or it may become too salty. Always rinse off the birds in plenty of cold water, then pat dry before cooking. Your brine can be made well in advance.

Brined and roasted quails with agresto sauce
pictured page 66

For the brined quail

3.5 litres (121 fl oz/14 cups) water
1 bunch of thyme
2 bay leaves
a good grinding of black pepper
280 g (10 oz/1¼ cups) salt
250 g (9 oz/heaped 1 cup) sugar
12 whole quails
about 200 g (7 oz) butter, at room
    temperature

To make the brine, pour the water into a large saucepan and bring to the boil. Add your herbs and pepper, then stir in the salt and sugar. As soon as the sugar and salt have dissolved, turn off the heat and allow to cool completely in the fridge.

Take your quails and clean any offal out of the cavity. When the brine is cold, add the quails to the brine and use a plate or cooling rack to weigh down the quails to ensure that they are totally submerged, then refrigerate for 3–4 hours.

Preheat your oven to 230°C (450°F/Gas 8). When you are ready to cook the birds, remove them from the brine and rinse in plenty of cold water, then pat dry. Take some of the butter in your hands and rub it all over the quails, then place them into a roasting tin. When you have all of the quails lined up, place them into the oven for about 30 minutes, or until they are nicely browned. Remove them from the oven and allow to rest upside down in the roasting tin for about another 10 minutes, which will be enough time to prepare your sauce.

For the agresto sauce

125 g (4½ oz/heaped ¾ cup) almonds
125 g (4½ oz/1¼ cups) walnuts
1 clove of garlic, chopped
1 bunch of flat-leaf (Italian) parsley, leaves finely
    chopped
½ bunch of basil, leaves finely chopped
80 ml (2½ fl oz/⅓ cup) extra virgin olive oil
80 ml (2½ fl oz/⅓ cup) verjuice
1 teaspoon salt
pepper

Place the nuts and the garlic into a food processor and blend finely, then transfer to a bowl and add your chopped herbs, olive oil and verjuice and mix really well—you should have a pasty 'pesto type' sauce. Now add your seasoning.

For serving

Once the quails have rested, you have the choice to either leave them whole or cut them. To cut them, place them onto a chopping board and insert the tip of a knife all the way into the cavity and cut down through the bottom of the bird. Turn the quail, breast side down, and open them up slightly, then cut through the middle of the breast. Remove the legs from the breast.

Place the whole quail or quail pieces into your bowl of sauce. Toss the quails around in the sauce to ensure that they are really well coated, then transfer to a platter. I like to serve the quail with the potatoes fried in red wine and coriander seeds (page 145).

Beef ribs smoked in watermelon

for six to share

A mate of mine, Jimmy, is a great cook, so when I was in his backyard for a barbecue and spied a platter of beautiful smoked beef ribs I was not surprised; after all, I have not eaten anything that Jimmy has cooked and been disappointed. It wasn't until I put some of the meat in my mouth that my world was blown apart—it was absolutely delicious! The most flavoursome, delicate, well-cooked piece of beef I think I have ever eaten. And there was this flavour that I couldn't put my finger on, which was so familiar ... so subtle, yet floral and fragrant ... it reminded me of kissing my wife just after she had applied lip gloss. Could it be? Surely not? Good God, I think this beef tastes like watermelon!

So like any good chef I unashamedly, and without a moment's hesitation, stole the recipe. I quite literally had a beef bone in my mouth while I was frantically yelling into my mobile phone, 'Order beef ribs, watermelon, ooh and some ginger. Do we have any allspice? Okay, well I need it first thing in the morning. Where can I get woodchips at 7 a.m. tomorrow?' I then went up to Jimmy and in an offhand, almost bored way said, 'Great beef man, what's in it?' My heart sank ... it took him 2 days to prepare the recipe, he had the meat slowly smoking in his kettle barbecue for about 13 hours and he used apple wood and fruit to do the smoking! I wanted to put it onto the menu the next night—I was a desperate man, so I came up with this recipe. I would never feel confident enough to compare this to Jimmy's ribs, but the result is delicious and has been a regular fixture on the bar food menu ever since.

I have given two cooking methods here: one is for a kettle barbecue and the other is for a normal kitchen oven. They both work well and have their own advantages and disadvantages. Cooking in your oven means that you won't get quite the same finish on the meat but it gives you much more control. However, my preference is for the barbecue for a couple of reasons; first, it is outside and you won't have your kitchen smelling of smoked meat and, second, because being a male the idea of cooking meat on a fire that I started fills me with a kind of primal pleasure.

1.25 kg (2 lb 12 oz) whole watermelon
a small knob of fresh ginger, peeled and grated
3 cloves of garlic, roughly chopped
5 whole allspice
1 piece of cinnamon stick
150 ml (5 fl oz) pomegranate molasses
6 ripe tomatoes, peeled, seeded and chopped
2 bay leaves
1 teaspoon chilli flakes
100 ml (3½ fl oz) olive oil
80 g (2¾ oz/⅓ cup) sugar
salt and ground black pepper
3 kg (6 lb 12 oz) square-cut beef ribs on the bone

Start by cutting the watermelon in half. Working over a large bowl, use a spoon to scrape out all of the watermelon flesh, removing any seeds as you are going along (a few seeds left are fine). Use a large whisk to mash the watermelon up while you are adding the remaining ingredients (except the ribs). Give it a taste—it should be slightly salty, slightly spicy and have a good balance between sweet and sour. You will get a much better result if you perfect the flavour now and allow the flavours to cook into the beef. Add your beef ribs to the marinade and let this sit in your fridge for at least 8 hours (but 24–48 hours is ideal). Here are two methods for cooking the ribs.

For the kettle barbecue method

The kettle barbecue will take up to 4½ hours to prepare your coals and cook the meat, making this a lazy Sunday cook-up. You will need to have fire starters, a bag of coal, small pieces of kindling and a bag of woodchips. The type of wood you use is up to you since different types of wood will impart different flavours, but do not use any treated or painted timber for obvious reasons.

Get a really good fire going at least 1½ hours before you want to cook your beef. When the flames have gone and the coals are good and hot, give them a bit of a stir around to ensure that they are evenly dispersed around the bottom of the barbecue—it will also allow some of the heat to escape from the coals. Now place small pieces of wood on top of the coals and leave the lid off the barbecue until you have a nice medium heat. The trick is to create an environment in which to cook your meat (about 140–160°C/275–315°F) that is filled with a nice gentle smoke. Place your hand above the coals to judge the heat—it should be hot but not searing. When you feel comfortable with the heat, take a few handfuls of woodchips that you have moistened with water (but not soaked) and sprinkle these around the bottom of the barbecue. Remove the ribs from the marinade and place on the grill plate of your barbecue over the hot coals. Spoon over some of the chunky bits of the marinade and cover with the lid. Check the barbecue every 20 minutes to baste the meat with some of the marinade and to ensure that the meat is not cooking too quickly and that there is a nice gentle smoke present, adding more woodchips if needed. Your meat will need to cook for up to 2½ hours and it is ready when the meat is nice and soft.

For the oven method

Preheat your oven to 200°C (400°F/Gas 6). You will need to have the following: a roasting tin that has a tight-fitting lid big enough to cover your meat, a small wire rack that you can fit in the bottom of the tin to keep the meat off the woodchips, and some woodchips. Start by soaking a couple of big handfuls of woodchips in water until they are nice and wet, then line the bottom of your roasting tin with foil. Spread out your moistened woodchips in the base of the tin, about 1 cm (½ in) thick. Place your roasting tin on a high heat on the stove and get your woodchips smoking quite hard. Turn off the heat and add the wire rack so it sits over the woodchips. Remove the ribs from the marinade and place on the rack. Spoon a small amount of the chunkier marinade pieces over the top of the ribs. Cover with the lid and then put straight into your oven. The cooking time is around 2½ hours and you need to check your meat about every 30 minutes to spoon over a little more marinade as it cooks.

For serving

I like to serve the meat with a big knife and cold beer, but I suppose a nice little salad might also be a good idea.

Hasselback potatoes with L'edel de cleron and a hazelnut dressing

for six to share

If you like a roasted potato, then the hasselback is a guaranteed winner! The way the potato is sliced gives it a wonderful texture with a satisfying crunch on the outside, and it allows all of the cheese and dressing to fall into the fluffy flesh of the potato. As far as how many potatoes to cook, I would allow at least three per person, but don't cook too many more unless you want to serve them on their own as they are quite rich. I like to use small cocktail potatoes for this as they make perfect one-bite mouthfuls.

The type of cheese you use is up to you—I prefer L'edel de cleron because, when ripe, it is rich and flavoursome while at the same time staying fairly delicate, but a brie or camembert would also work well here. L'edel de cleron is a soft, ripened Vacherin-style cheese with a white mould rind. One thing that many people do not understand is that cheese, like any good produce, ripens as it ages and has a peak period when it is at its best. Depending on the type of cheese, once it reaches this point it will last for a couple of days or a couple of months. Make friends with your local cheesemonger and you'll soon experience the joy of eating cheese at its best.

Hasselback potatoes with L'edel de cleron and a hazelnut dressing

pictured page 72

For the toasted hazelnut dressing

100 g (3½ oz/¾ cup) hazelnuts
½ clove of garlic
60 ml (2 fl oz/¼ cup) extra virgin
  olive oil
½ lemon, zest cut into strips, juiced
salt and ground black pepper
small pinch of sugar

Preheat your oven to 120°C (235°F/Gas ½). Lay the hazelnuts onto a baking tray and lightly bake for 10–12 minutes, or just until you see the skins start to split and the nut take on a little colour. One thing to know about toasting hazelnuts is that they will take more colour in the centre of the nut than on the outside, so if you are cooking by eye (that is, looking at the colour of the nut) you should always cook them a little less than you would for other nuts. When you are happy with the nuts, tip them out onto a dry tea towel (dish towel) and wrap them; let them sit like this for a moment and then gently rub to loosen all of the skins from the nut—if a few little shards of skin remain attached to the nut, this is fine.

Carefully remove the hazelnuts from the tea towel and place them onto a chopping board. Use the flat of a knife to crack the hazelnuts into rough pieces; while you are doing this, take your clove of garlic and squash it with the flat of your knife but leave in one piece.

Place the hazelnuts into a frying pan with the garlic, olive oil and 3 or 4 strips of lemon. Place your pan onto a high heat and cook until everything has fried a little, about 4–5 minutes. When you are happy with the beautiful golden colour on the nuts and garlic and the room has a delicious warming hazelnut aroma, remove your pan from the heat and add the juice from your lemon. Taste for seasoning, adding more lemon juice if required, then adding salt, pepper and sugar—the aim is for a well-balanced vinaigrette. Leave the dressing at room temperature.

For the potatoes

3–4 potatoes per person (the best potatoes to
  use are a small cocktail potato such as chat
  or nicola)
butter, at room temperature
salt and ground black pepper

Preheat your oven to 220°C (425°F/Gas 7). Look at your potato to see how you want it presented; if there is a slight mark, make that the bottom of your potato. Slice off a little from the bottom of the potato so they can stand up without wobbling. Now comes the fiddly bit. The best knife to use to 'hasselback' the potatoes is one that is sharp and thin. Place the potato on your chopping board, cut side down. Starting at one end, slice the potato almost all the way down but not through the base. Make parallel cuts 1 mm (¹⁄₃₂ in) apart all the way along the potato. Repeat with the rest of the potatoes. Place your potatoes on a greased baking tray and rub each potato with plenty of butter, then season with salt and pepper.

Place the potatoes into the oven and roast for about 30 minutes; halfway through the cooking process, brush the potatoes with a little more butter. The potatoes are cooked when you have a nice golden crust and they are tender in the centre when tested with a knife.

For serving

1 wheel L'edel de cleron or other beautiful
  Vacherin-style cheese
salt and ground black pepper

While the potatoes are still hot, place them onto a platter and spoon a generous amount of the cheese over them. Drizzle with some of the hazelnut dressing, being sure to mound some of the nuts on top. Season with a little more salt and ground black pepper and serve as soon as possible.

Casserole of pork belly, pancetta and clams

for eight to share

I know this sounds like a pretty crazy combination but it works incredibly well. There is a little bit of preparation involved and you have to start the day before. When you look over the recipe you will see that it also involves marinating the pork in milk overnight, but please don't be put off—take a chance and you won't be disappointed. With this dish you will be cooking three different things at the same time, so do what you can to be prepared and have all your ingredients on hand before you start to cook. You will also need to have a large heavy-based casserole dish with a tight-fitting lid to cook this dish.

For the pork belly

1 kg (2 lb 4 oz) piece of pork belly off the bone, skin removed
100 ml (3½ fl oz) dry white wine
500 ml (17 fl oz/2 cups) milk
4 bay leaves
salt and ground black pepper

Take the pork belly and cut it into 1.5 cm (⅝ in) cubes and place it in a bowl with the white wine, milk, bay leaves and a little salt and a good grinding of black pepper. Cover with plastic wrap and let it sit in the fridge overnight.

For the clams

1.5 kg (3 lb 5 oz) surf clams or vongole

You will want to make sure that you purge your clams to ensure they are free from grit. To do this, place them into a large container of tap water with a little salt added and let them sit for a day in your fridge. The next day, rinse the clams really well in plenty of cold water.

For the potatoes

6 (about 750 g/1 lb 10 oz) pontiac potatoes or sweet waxy potatoes
olive oil
salt and ground black pepper
1 bulb of garlic, unpeeled, cut in half crossways
a few sprigs of thyme
2 bay leaves

Preheat your oven to 180°C (450°F/Gas 4). Start by cooking your potatoes; this first step can even be done the day before. Place the potatoes on a roasting tray, drizzle with a little olive oil, season with salt and pepper and add your garlic, thyme and bay leaves. Cover with foil and bake for about 50 minutes, or until the potatoes are tender when tested with a knife. Remove the potatoes from the oven and lift off the foil. Discard the garlic, thyme and bay leaves. They can now be stored in the fridge overnight, if you want to prepare them earlier, or you can continue with the next step straight away.

Use the back of a spoon to squash the potatoes flat so that they almost cover the whole pan. Add a little more olive oil, place the roasting tray on your stovetop over two hobs and start to gently fry on a gentle heat. When they are well coloured, turn them over and fry the other side—this will take 20–30 minutes in total and you may need to add a little more oil.

For the tomatoes

    8 ripe roma (plum) tomatoes
    salt and ground black pepper
    a drizzle of olive oil
    1 clove of garlic, crushed

Cut the tomatoes in half and place on a roasting tray, cut side down. Season with a little salt and pepper, drizzle with a little olive oil and add the garlic.

Cook the tomatoes in the oven at the same time as you are roasting the pork. Roast for about 20 minutes, or until the skins start to blister, then remove from the oven, pinch off the tomato skins and transfer the flesh to a bowl and squash them to a purée.

For the casserole

    your marinated pork belly
    a good slug of olive oil
    185 g (6½ oz) pancetta, cut into lardons
        (short 5 mm/¼ in wide batons)
    3 cloves of garlic, crushed
    8 French shallots, thinly sliced
    your cleaned clams
    the mashed, cooked tomatoes
    200 ml (7 fl oz) vermouth
    350 ml (12 fl oz) chicken stock
    1 bunch of thyme
    a sprinkling of chopped flat-leaf (Italian) parsley

Preheat your oven to 180°C (350°F/Gas 4). To start the casserole you need to drain off the pork belly, rinse it really well and then pat dry. Now place a large flameproof casserole dish onto the top of your stove on a high heat and pour in a good slug of olive oil. When the oil is nice and hot, add your pieces of pork. Fry the pork in batches for a while to get a good brown colour, turning the pieces from time to time. Transfer the casserole dish to the oven. (Now is the time to roast the tomatoes.) After about 30 minutes the pork should have a beautiful roasted aroma and be just starting to soften up when you insert the tip of your knife. This dish is supposed to be rich and fatty, but you may want to tip off a little of the fat at this stage.

Lift the dish back onto the top of your stove over a medium heat and add the pancetta, garlic and shallots. Stir well and allow the pancetta and garlic to colour slightly, then add your clams and stir really well. Now add the puréed tomatoes and vermouth and cover with a lid until the clams have steamed open, which will take about 5 minutes. Take off the lid and add the chicken stock and thyme and gently simmer for a couple of moments. Taste your broth for seasoning and adjust if needed; when you are completely happy with everything, stir in your chopped parsley and take to the table with your fried potatoes on the side.

Strawberry breast

for four

The first time I saw this recipe was when I happened to flick to the Discovery Channel and started to watch a program about Sicily and Saint Agatha. I was surprised to see a procession of large platters of huge pink breasts being carried through the streets by hoards of people. I was a little amused to say the least when I then watched one of the breasts placed onto a large table to be portioned up for everyone to have a piece. I did a little research and discovered a wonderful dessert called 'Fragomammella'. The story (and there are a few versions) is that Saint Agatha, after refusing advances from the local magistrate 'Quinctianus', was forced into a brothel and tortured. Her torture included having her breasts removed and being refused medical care until Saint Peter appeared before her and allowed her to die. Not the nicest story but I do have to say that while I was learning about poor Saint Agatha I did find myself constantly thinking, 'This is a great dessert, I can't wait to get it on the menu'. I have altered it slightly from the original recipe by adding just a little goat's cheese to the cream—traditionally, it should be ricotta.

For the strawberries

500 g (1 lb 2 oz) strawberries
2 tablespoons water
1 lemon, peeled then juiced, peel reserved
250 g (9 oz/heaped 1 cup) caster (superfine)
    sugar

You want to cook the strawberries a couple of hours in advance or even the day before. Start by rinsing the strawberries, then shake off most of the water—a little bit of water will actually help you cook the strawberries. Remove the green tops and sort through the strawberries, cutting any large ones in half.

Pour the water and juice from the lemon into a large flat frying pan, then add the sugar and place onto a medium heat and cook until the sugar has melted and dissolved. During this process try not to stir the sugar too much, instead swirl the pan around to move the sugar about. When the sugar has started to cook, turn your heat up high and cook just until you start to get a little colour, then add the strawberries and lemon peel. The sugar will set and clump on the strawberries which is fine—try to coat the strawberries as well as you can in the hot caramel, then remove the pan from the heat and scrape everything into a bowl.

As the strawberries cool after a couple of hours, strain off the juice and discard the lemon peel. Place the strawberries in the fridge and pour the remaining juice into a small saucepan and boil until it has reduced by half, then remove from the heat and allow to cool completely in the fridge.

For the cream

200 ml (7 fl oz) thick (double/heavy) cream
80 g (2¾ oz) soft goat's cheese
80 ml (2½ fl oz/⅓ cup) of the chilled
    strawberry syrup

You want to make the cream close to serving but it will sit for about an hour or so in the fridge. Place the cream in a large bowl, then crumble your goat's cheese into the smallest pieces you can manage, and add to the bowl. Use a large whisk to fold the cheese through the cream until you just start to see ribbons. Drizzle in the cold strawberry syrup to give you a soft pink hue. Use a whisk to whip until you have soft peaks but don't worry if the cheese is not completely incorporated, as you don't want to overwork the cream.

For serving

2–3 leaves of mint

Make a mound of strawberries on a platter while reserving one strawberry that looks best. Take the mint and tear into little pieces and scatter over the strawberries. Now take your cream and using the biggest serving spoon you have, dip it in hot water and then try to get one large scoop of cream to cover the strawberries. You should have a little of the strawberry syrup left so pour a little around the 'breast'. To finish, place on the last remaining strawberry … you guessed it, the nipple.

Fresh berries with crème de framboise and clotted cream

for four to six

I think that we are all familiar with fresh berries, aren't we? Well then, what about clotted cream? I know the name doesn't exactly sound appealing but, trust me, it is fantastic. It has the texture of soft butter and a wonderful slightly waxy and buttery flavour. The best thing is that the less you do to it the better—in fact, if you try to mix the cream too much it will lose its natural thick but light consistency. Clotted cream is made by taking the cream from Jersey cows (the milk from the Jersey cow has a higher fat content than the milk from other cows) and gently scalding the cream, then allowing it to cool slowly so that it can form a yellow, wrinkly and crusty surface. It is normally sold in shallow trays and when you serve it, simply scoop from the tub, but be sure to serve some of the fabulous crust with each scoop.

There is no trick or mystery to this dish—the only surprise is how good the combination of berries and clotted cream can be. You should only buy berries that you have had an opportunity to sample first to ensure that their flavour is worthy enough, but the type of berries you select is completely up to you. If all you can get is strawberries then so be it; if you can get hold of a wide selection of beautiful berries then all the better. I like to use crème de framboise to marinate the berries but you can substitute this for any berry-flavoured liquor.

550 g (1 lb 4 oz) fresh berries
150 ml (5 fl oz) crème de framboise
a touch of sugar
a few leaves of mint
150 g (5½ oz) clotted cream (or as much as you want!)

Do as little as possible to the berries (such as removing the green tops from the strawberries) and only cut them if it is absolutely necessary. All you need to do is place your berries into a large bowl, then pour in the crème de framboise, add a little sugar and then sprinkle in a few mint leaves. Gently toss to ensure that the berries are well coated and leave this in the fridge for an hour or two. When you are ready to serve, either spoon the berries into individual dishes or pour into a large serving bowl, making sure to drizzle in all of the liquor, then top with dollops of the clotted cream.

Baked ricotta with cherries in a vanilla syrup

pictured page 80

for eight

This is a simple dessert that can be prepared in advance, then all that is left to do is to serve. It is a good recipe to master as it opens the door to loads of variations—during spring it is great with stone fruits, but in the cooler months try tamarillos or citrus fruit. You can also try folding different nuts through the ricotta. This version is my personal favourite—I just love the colour and flavour.

For the baked ricotta

750 g (1 lb 10 oz/3 cups) ricotta cheese
2 eggs
1 vanilla bean
175 g (6 oz/$^3/_4$ cup) caster (superfine) sugar
200 g (7 oz/1$^1/_3$ cups) unsalted pistachio nuts

Preheat your oven to 150°C (300°F/Gas 2). Put the ricotta and eggs in a large bowl, then beat together. Carefully split the vanilla bean and scrape the seeds into the ricotta, reserving the bean itself for the syrup. Now add the sugar and pistachios and beat together well.

Life is easier if you use a non-stick loaf (bar) tin, about 21 x 10 x 5 cm (8$^1/_4$ x 4 x 2 in), for the ricotta, but if you don't have a non-stick tin, then grease and line the tin with plastic wrap. Spoon the ricotta mixture into the tin and smooth the top, then cover the tin with foil.

You now want to cook the ricotta in a bain-marie, which basically means in a water bath. To do this, place your loaf tin into a larger tin or roasting tray and pour in enough boiling water to come halfway up the outside of the ricotta tin. Bake this for 50 minutes. Remove from the water, take off the foil and allow the ricotta to cool completely in the fridge before turning out—it will need a few hours to cool.

For the cherries

280 g (10 oz/1$^1/_4$ cups) sugar
1 lemon
the leftover vanilla bean from the ricotta
100 ml (3$^1/_2$ fl oz) cold water
55 ml (1$^3/_4$ fl oz) kirsch
250 g (9 oz) cherries

Put the sugar, a small piece of lemon zest, the vanilla bean and water in a saucepan and cook over medium heat for about 10 minutes, or until you have a very pale caramel. Remove the pan from the heat and stop the cooking process by carefully adding a squeeze of lemon juice and the kirsch. Allow to cool completely but don't refrigerate—it will take about 45 minutes.

Take your cherries and remove their stems. Working over a bowl, tear the cherries in half to remove the stone. I like the look of the torn untidy pieces of cherry; also you will be squeezing out the juice, which will look great on the plate. Keep in the fridge until you are ready to serve.

For serving

Slice the ricotta into about eight even pieces, depending on how many people you are serving. Remove the lemon zest and vanilla bean from the syrup and pour the syrup over the cherries, then serve the cherries over the cut ricotta.

The best chocolate cake recipe I know

for sixteen

While I have been writing this book I have had this recipe in my head and a little voice has been saying, 'Noooooo, keep this one secret ... don't tell anyone how to make it'. In fact, I even know of a chef who had his staff sign non-disclosure agreements before handing them this recipe (sorry, but the cat is now out of the bag).

This cake has all of the bases covered—it is chocolate, it is rich, it is fabulous! But there is a catch. It cannot be eaten on the same day it is made; you must show a little restraint when making it. The other small catch is that you must use really good chocolate. I am not being a food snob or anything (I'll be the first one to crave a dodgy chocolate bar after a great meal), but the simple reality is that cooking chocolate or white chocolate will not work—trust me on this as I have tried (in vain) to short-cut this recipe but it is just not the same.

The cooking times and temperatures are quite precise and worth following the first time, but you will probably find that the second time you make this recipe it will be better, as you will be able to make little changes to the times and temperature to suit your own oven. If you need any advice about how to adjust the recipe to your oven, please contact me and I'm happy to help.

The best chocolate cake recipe I know

pictured page 81

butter, for greasing

plain (all-purpose) flour, for dusting

500 g (1 lb 2 oz) Callebaut '811' chocolate callets (buttons) or a good-quality dark chocolate with around 53% cocoa solids, chopped

250 g (9 oz) unsalted butter, chopped

10 eggs

a pinch of salt

50 g (1¾ oz/¼ cup) caster (superfine) sugar

35 g (1¼ oz/¼ cup) plain (all-purpose) flour

Preheat your oven to 205°C (400°F/Gas 6). Now prepare a 22 cm (8½ in) spring-form cake tin by rubbing with a little butter and dusting with flour. Have ready a lightly greased (but not floured) flat ovenproof dinner plate that will be large enough to sit over the edges of your tin.

Put the chocolate and butter in a clean heatproof bowl, then place the bowl over a saucepan of simmering water, without letting the base of the bowl touch the water. Gently melt the chocolate. While this is happening, start to carefully separate your eggs, placing the yolks in one small bowl and the whites into a large bowl or the bowl of an electric mixer with a whisking attachment (if you prefer, you can whisk the whites by hand using a balloon whisk and brute force, but an electric mixer will make the job much easier).

When the chocolate and butter have melted, add a pinch of salt, stir well and remove from the heat to allow it to cool slightly. While this is happening, start to whisk your egg whites. When your egg whites have formed soft peaks, sprinkle in the sugar and continue to whisk for about 1 more minute until the sugar has dissolved and the whites take on a nice shine. Now add the flour to the egg yolks and mix thoroughly.

You now need a clean large bowl in which to mix everything. Start by pouring in your melted chocolate mixture, then, using a whisk, beat in your egg yolk and flour mixture really well. Now, using your hands, fold your egg white mixture into the chocolate, one-third at a time, being careful to combine everything, but do not overwork. Working quickly, pour the chocolate batter into your prepared tin, then place into the oven for 15 minutes. After 15 minutes gently place the prepared plate, greased side down, on top of the cake tin (by now the cake will have started to rise) and put the tin back into the oven for 12 minutes. Once the cooking time has finished, resist the urge to lift the plate (but if you do and the cake looks unset and runny, don't panic, this is what it is supposed to look like) and place the cake (still in its tin, covered by the plate) on a wire rack out of direct sunlight, in a cool spot for at least 24 hours.

For serving

The next day carefully lift off the dinner plate. You will find that the cake will have sunk in the middle and will look a little ugly, but do not judge a book by its cover because you are about to have a wonderful chocolate experience. Carefully unclip and remove the side of the spring-form tin. Use a knife that has been heated in hot water and then dried to cut slices of your cake and simply serve with fresh tart berries and cream. Your cake should have the texture of a smooth and exotic pâté.

Do not place the cake in the fridge as it will sit at room temperature for about 2 days. Enjoy.

Autumn menu for a shared table

Jared's martini

for one

There is no other drink subject to more scrutiny and attention than the martini. It is said to be the most consumed cocktail in the world and there are variations for everyone, from the simple classic martini (gin-based) to the dry martini, very dry martini, dirty martini or martini with a twist, which are all made up of basically the same ingredients but have quite different flavours. Then there is the gibson, a martini garnished with a cocktail onion, which changes the flavour of the drink so dramatically that it has been given a completely different name. The recipe and method I give here is for how I like *my* martini. Rather than give you a list of recipes for different variations, I will instead explain how the flavours work and in that way, through experimentation, you will be able to find *your* favourite. I will offer a word of caution that is best summed up in a quote I once heard, 'One martini is not enough. Two martinis are too many. Three martinis are not enough'.

To begin, your gin must be well chilled; in fact, it is best to keep it in the freezer—icy cold gin is a smoother and much more appealing drink. The type of gin that you use is completely up to you. Some gins claim to be the perfect 'martini gin' while others taste like a combination of petrol and ear wax! Some bartenders will tell you that the more you pay for your gin, the better it will be—this is a very general rule as it really does come down to personal preference and, unfortunately, you are just going to have to experiment until you find the one you like best.

Vermouth is a fortified wine flavoured with herbs and spices. Its name is derived from a German fortified wine that was made with *wermut* or wormwood, which is the key ingredient in absinthe. The less vermouth used, the drier the finish; more vermouth makes the drink 'wetter'. The classic martini has a ratio of four parts gin to one part vermouth. If you don't use your vermouth very often, it is best to keep it in the fridge as it does lose its aroma and flavour over time.

The ice is very important—it needs to be clean and very frozen, not watery, so never use crushed ice for a martini. The ice plays such an important role that I know of people who buy pure distilled water to make their own ice as they believe that tap water gives an unsatisfactory flavour to their martinis.

As for the olive, this is really up to you, but do not use a black olive, only a green olive. My favourite is the gordal olive, which is a large green olive that is quite fleshy and crunchy in texture and tends to have a clean saltiness to it.

You should always serve a martini in a martini glass. Some people say that a martini glass plays a very important role in the way a martini tastes, evaporates, swirls or some other nonsense. For me, it's a matter of tradition: serving a martini in anything other than a martini glass is like drawing a moustache on the *Mona Lisa*—it would be destroying a classic!

10 ml (2 teaspoons) vermouth
60 ml (2 fl oz/¼ cup) gin
ice
1 green olive

In a cocktail shaker, combine the vermouth and gin with plenty of ice, place on the cap to the shaker and gently shake three or four times to ensure that everything is well chilled. If you shake too much you will be diluting the drink with water and some puritans would say that over shaking can 'bruise' your gin. Double-strain your martini into a chilled martini glass and add your olive.

Negroni
for one

A wonderful Spanish aperitif that would usually be served at the beginning of the meal, but I also like to sip mine while enjoying a dessert, such as the Sour cherry and apple parfait (page 123). I love the contrast between the sweetness of the dessert and the bitterness of the drink.

1 slice of orange, with peel
ice
20 ml (½ fl oz) gin
20 ml (½ fl oz) Campari
20 ml (½ fl oz) sweet vermouth

Place the orange into your glass and crush slightly with the back of your cocktail spoon, add ice and stir well before adding the alcohol.

Quince royale

for one

This is a play on the classic kir royale, which is cassis and Champagne. It was named after Félix Kir who, when he was the Mayor of Dijon, offered the drink at receptions for visiting delegates. I love serving this drink before a dinner and it is also a really good way of using up the syrup from your cooked quinces (page 120), though you will need to reduce the syrup before using it in this cocktail, which means that it is really more suitable to prepare for groups than for just one person.

30 ml (1 fl oz) quince syrup (page 120)
100 ml (3½ fl oz) Champagne

Place the syrup in a saucepan, bring to the boil and reduce by half. Chill completely before using.

This is a very simple drink to prepare—you can set up your champagne flutes with the quince syrup ready and waiting for when your guests arrive and then simply top up with the Champagne.

Persimmon and sake martini

for four

pictured page 91

For this, I prefer to use fuyu persimmons, which have a far superior flavour to other persimmons when they are very ripe; if you are unfamiliar with this type of persimmon you would probably think that they were overripe. The problem is that once they are at this stage they can become overripe very quickly, which would irritate me to no end. I used to try to think of all sorts of elaborate uses for overripe persimmons—that is until I read a line in a cookbook by Suzanne Goin that stated that, 'A frozen persimmon has the texture of sorbet'. At Danks Street Depot we often go to great lengths to make easy things difficult, so a sorbet recipe as easy as, 'Place whole fruit in the freezer' seemed a little too good to be true, but we gave it a go and wouldn't you know, it not only worked but was delicious; in fact, overripe fruit has more concentrated sugars, which give your sorbet a better flavour and consistency. It is about as easy a sorbet as you will ever get. This drink/dessert is a great way to finish a meal, but I have also served it as a drink on its own.

1 persimmon

50 g (1¾ oz/⅓ cup) shaved palm sugar
    (jaggery)

60 ml (2 fl oz/¼ cup) tequila

325 ml (11 fl oz) sake

You want to have your persimmon in the freezer for at least a day to allow it to freeze completely; it will keep quite well in there for a couple of weeks. So my suggestion is to freeze persimmons once they are overripe and leave them in there until you need them.

Take your persimmon out of the freezer and let it sit at room temperature for a couple of minutes before attempting to handle it. You now want to cut the frozen fruit. Please take great care when doing this as it will be easy for the knife to slip and for you to cut yourself. Cut the fruit into quarters and then into slices about 2 mm (¹⁄₁₆ in) thick.

Place the slices of persimmon into a large cocktail shaker, then add the palm sugar, tequila and sake and, using a large spoon, break the persimmon into chunks. Combine the mixture, then pour it into a martini glass and serve with a spoon.

Pretzels with walnut 'butter'

makes 16 pretzels, great for a nibble

I love pretzels, either straight from the oven or crisp and dried out a few days later. They are a great thing to make with kids as the dough is very simple and forgiving and you can come up with all sorts of fun and interesting shapes. I like to serve these at Danks Street Depot at the start of a meal with just a little spiced walnut 'butter'. But if you are going to have a big meal, make the pretzels smaller as they are incredibly moreish and if you don't show some restraint you can easily fill up on these and ruin your meal.

Pretzels have an interesting history. In the year AD 610 (so the story goes), an Italian monk took scraps of dough, rolled them into little logs and twisted them to depict arms crossed in prayer. He then called them *pretiolas*, which translates as 'little gifts' as they were used to reward children for remembering their night-time prayers. We now know them as pretzels and I reckon that they are just perfect with lashings of beer, which I could argue is very much like my night-time prayer

For the pretzels

900 g (2 lb/7¼ cups) plain (all-purpose) flour
60 g (2¼ oz/⅓ cup) soft brown sugar
2 teaspoons salt
1 tablespoon dried yeast
1 tablespoon warm water, plus 500 ml
    (17 fl oz/2 cups) warm water
750 ml (26 fl oz/3 cups) boiling water
1 tablespoon bicarbonate of soda (baking soda)
sea salt and sesame seeds or your favourite
    sprinkles

Combine the flour, sugar and salt in a large bowl, then make a well in the centre. In a bowl, mix the yeast with 1–2 tablespoons of the water to dissolve the yeast; let it sit for a brief moment. Pour the remaining water into your yeast mixture, then pour this mixture into the well made in your flour. Start combining all of the liquid into your flour until it has just come together, then continue to knead the dough while still in the bowl until it becomes nice and smooth. Cover the dough with a damp cloth and leave to prove in a warm place for about 30 minutes, or until it doubles in size. Preheat your oven to 230°C (450°F/Gas 8). Lightly grease a baking tray.

'Knock back' your dough by kneading it once more and then divide your dough into 16 even pieces, about the size of a golf ball. Start shaping your dough by rolling it into thin sausages of dough about 30 cm (12 in) long.

I find that when I am making pretzels at home it takes me about 2 minutes to roll and shape a pretzel, so I find it easiest to shape each pretzel one at a time, then cook them one at a time while I shape the next.

To shape a pretzel, create a loop with the rolled dough and overlap so that each end has about an 8 cm (3¼ inch) overhang. Twist the dough to seal this join and flip the knot back toward the curve of the loop to form a figure eight.

In a saucepan, combine the boiling water and bicarbonate of soda, bring back to the boil, then drop your pretzels in the boiling water for about 2 minutes until they start to rise to the surface. Remove them from the water and put them straight onto your greased baking tray. Sprinkle them with your favourite flavouring, such as sea salt and sesame seeds, then bake in the oven for about 12 minutes, or until nice and golden, in batches if necessary.

For the spiced walnut 'butter'

400 g (14 oz/4 cups) shelled walnuts (The best walnut will come from walnuts that you shell yourself in autumn or early winter. You can use pre-shelled walnuts, but be warned: once you use fresh walnuts you will never go back!)
1 teaspoon salt
a pinch of sugar
a pinch of chilli powder, optional
125 ml (4 fl oz/½ cup) walnut oil

Put everything in a blender. You can leave out the chilli if you prefer, but I like the gentle heat it adds to the butter, making it work well as a savoury spread. Blend the ingredients, taking care to scrape down the side of the blender from time to time. Keep blending until it has formed a paste and from there simply blend until you have the texture you want—smooth or crunchy, which are you?

This butter will keep well in the fridge for about a month but just remember to remove it from the fridge to soften before you use it. As the butter settles, the oil will pool on top, simply stir it back in before you use it, don't pour it off as it will keep the butter nice and moist.

For serving

Place a dish of the spiced walnut 'butter' alongside the plate of pretzels for spreading.

Chickpea purée

for eight as a nibble

You can use precooked and tinned chickpeas for this recipe but the flavour will not be anywhere near as good as if you soak and cook your own chickpeas. When you buy dried chickpeas they should be pale and intact. Sort through your chickpeas and remove any discoloured and dark brown chickpeas. If you want to make this dip even more special, then use a really good extra virgin olive oil—something nice and peppery.

220 g (7¾ oz/1 cup) dried chickpeas, soaked in
    cold water for 24 hours
2 tablespoons freshly ground cumin
150 g (5½ oz) tahini
juice of 2 lemons
salt and ground black pepper
115–150 ml (3¾–5 fl oz) extra virgin
    olive oil

Boil the chickpeas in plenty of cold water for at least 2½ hours, or until the chickpeas are very tender. It is very important not to salt the water at all or the chickpeas will not become tender no matter how much you cook them.

When the chickpeas are cooked, drain them, reserving about 60 ml (2 fl oz/¼ cup) of the cooking liquid. Place the chickpeas in a blender and process with the reserved cooking liquid until smooth, then add the cumin, tahini, most of the lemon juice and some salt and pepper. While the blender is running, slowly pour in 115 ml (3¾ fl oz) of olive oil, then stop the blender and taste for seasoning and consistency. When you are tasting, keep in mind that the cumin flavour will become slightly stronger as it sits, and that the consistency should be soft. If you think it needs the remainder of the oil and lemon juice, add it now. The dip is ready to serve but if you want a much finer purée, then pass through the smallest plate on a mouli.

For serving
a drizzle of extra virgin olive oil
flat bread crackers (page 54) or crackers of
    your choice
wedges of lemon

To serve, place a dollop of the chickpea purée on a plate, make a well in the centre and drizzle in some oil. Serve alongside crackers and wedges of lemon.

Slow-cooked broccoli and bitter greens pie

for six to eight to share

Before you even think about starting this recipe, you need to put to one side all common thinking about cooking broccoli. You need to get your head around the fact that you will not be cooking the broccoli briefly in order to keep it bright and crunchy—instead you will be cooking your broccoli slowly until it becomes quite soft. Now before you go rolling your eyes skyward and thinking I have gone crazy, slow-cooked broccoli does not mean overcooked broccoli. What it does mean is that you will be cooking your vegetable until it transforms into something quite brilliant. It has a really rich, warm and nutty flavour that lends itself to an old-fashioned hearty pie. I have paired the broccoli with a couple of other greens here but you can easily substitute any of these for something else; I often use turnip tops or beetroot (beet) tops.

When buying broccoli it is (unfortunately) usually found with only a small amount of stem poking out from under the flowers. If you are lucky enough either to grow your own broccoli or have a good greengrocer who will get you broccoli with as much stem left on as possible, you will have a much better result. The flavour and texture of the broccoli stem is absolutely delicious—as it was described in an American gardening journal from 1800, the broccoli flower eats like cauliflower, but the stem eats like asparagus. The last word of advice is to buy young, small heads of broccoli because if broccoli is left on the plant too long, the stems will become tough and fibrous.

For the olive oil pastry

280 g (10 oz/2¼ cups) plain (all-purpose) flour
½ teaspoon salt
1½ tablespoons olive oil
135 ml (4½ fl oz) water

Combine the flour and salt in a large bowl and make a well in the centre, then add the olive oil and water and form into a firm dough, adding a little more water if it is too dry. Wrap your dough up really well in a piece of plastic wrap and let this rest for at least 2 hours in the fridge, then keep at room temperature for a few minutes before rolling the pastry. Resting the dough makes it a lot easier to work with—if you try rolling the dough straight away, you will find it rubbery and hard to work with.

For the filling

1 large head of broccoli (about 400 g/14 oz)
2 onions, finely diced
125 ml (4 fl oz/½ cup) olive oil
2 large red chillies, split and seeded
plenty of salt and ground black pepper
100 ml (3½ fl oz) dry white wine
1 large bunch of rapini (broccoli raab) or
    silverbeet (Swiss chard)
2 potatoes, boiled in their skins, peeled
    and diced into 1 cm (½ in) cubes
1 large handful of rocket (arugula), coarsely
    chopped
1 large handful of flat-leaf (Italian) parsley,
    chopped
a touch of fresh marjoram
4 eggs, lightly beaten together

Start by preparing the broccoli. Trim only the very bottom of the stem, leaving on as much of the stem as possible, then use a vegetable peeler to remove the fibrous thick green skin from the lower portion of the broccoli stem. Cut the broccoli lengthways into about eight evenly sized wedges.

In a large saucepan, combine the onion and about half of the olive oil and cook over a low heat until the onion is nice and soft, but does not colour. Add the chilli and broccoli, season well with salt and pepper and splash in the white wine. Cover your pan and cook over a very low heat for about 30 minutes, stirring very gently from time to time. The broccoli is ready when it is completely soft. Preheat your oven to 190°C (375°F/Gas 5).

While the broccoli is cooking, wilt the other greens. If you are using rapini, then simply cut the leafy ends into 2–3 cm (¾–1¼ in) pieces; if you are using silverbeet, remove the white stem and chop the leaves. You will need to wilt the greens in batches; do this by placing some of your leaves into a large flat pan with a drizzle of the olive oil and a little water, gently cook until they have become nice and soft, then transfer to a bowl to cool. When all of the leaves are cooked and cooled, use your hands to squeeze out as much of the liquid as possible, then place into a clean bowl with the potato, rocket, herbs and eggs. When the broccoli is cooked, gently lift it out and set aside; mix the onion and cooking juices into the greens and potato mixture.

For the pie

oil, for greasing
200 g (7 oz) feta cheese, crumbled

Grease a 28 cm (11¼ in) pie tin. Roll out the pastry until it is large enough to fit into your tin, with a little hanging over the edges, and allow this to rest for another 30 minutes. Pinch off the excess pastry hanging over the edges, then place in all of your filling—your broccoli will mush up a little but that is okay, just try to be gentle so you get as much in one piece as possible. Crumble the feta over the top, then bake the pie for about 45 minutes.

Beef cheek burgers with cabbage and beetroot
makes six burgers

For the crépinette (patties)

1 kg (2 lb 4 oz) beef cheeks, trimmed of
    excess fat
a little seasoned plain (all-purpose) flour
duck fat or oil, for frying
1 kg (2 lb 4 oz) onions, finely diced
2 cloves of garlic, chopped
a few sprigs of thyme
salt and ground black pepper
600 ml (21 fl oz) red wine
stock (any type) or water, optional
2 tablespoons hot mustard
a few sprigs of flat-leaf (Italian) parsley,
    leaves chopped
400 g (14 oz) fresh pork caul

Preheat your oven to 180°C (350°F/Gas 4). Start by placing a large flameproof casserole dish on a high heat. Lightly coat the beef cheeks in a little flour and fry them in the duck fat or oil until they are a good brown colour. Remove the cheeks from the dish and tip off any burnt or excess oil—do not wipe your dish but instead add a little more fresh fat or oil. Return the dish to the heat and cook the onion with the garlic, thyme, salt and pepper until the onion is soft, then return your cheeks to the dish and add all of the wine. The cheeks need to be completely covered, so you may need to add a little stock or water.

Bring this to the boil on your stove, then cover with a tight-fitting lid before moving to your oven to gently braise the cheeks for at least 2 hours, or until the cheeks have become completely soft. During the cooking process you will need to turn the cheeks from time to time to ensure even cooking.

When they are completely cooked, remove them from the liquid and pour the liquid into a container to be used when cooking the crépinette. When cool enough to handle, shred the meat and place into a large bowl, then add the mustard, parsley and seasoning.

Now you want to wrap the filling in caul. Start by rinsing the caul in plenty of cold water. Take hold of a piece and unravel a nice large sheet of the caul and place onto your chopping board. Using one-sixth of the beef mixture, form a ball and shape it into a rough patty shape before placing onto the caul—it won't shrink too much during the next stage of cooking so this will be pretty much the same size as the finished crépinette. Take up the edges of the caul to wrap the filling completely, trimming away any excess caul. Repeat with the remaining caul and beef. Refrigerate until ready to cook.

For the beetroot

about 1 kg (2 lb 4 oz) table salt
4 large beetroots (beets), skins on and leaves
    removed
salt and ground black pepper
a splash of truffle oil
a splash of olive oil

Preheat your oven to 180°C (350°F/Gas 4). On a baking tray, lay down a bed of salt, nestle in the beetroots and then bake for about 25 minutes, or until the beetroots are tender when tested with a knife. When they are cooked, remove the beetroots from the salt and set to one side until they are cool enough to handle but before they get completely cold. Wearing gloves, scrape away the skin from the beetroots. Slice the beetroot about 5 mm (1/4 in) thick and then place into a small bowl, season with salt and pepper and add a little truffle oil and olive oil. The beetroots are best if they are done a couple of hours in advance and then left out at room temperature.

For the buttered cabbage

1/2 small savoy cabbage
a knob of butter
salt and ground black pepper

You only really need enough cabbage to fill your burgers so, depending on the size of your cabbage, you may not need it all. Shred the cabbage as finely as you can with a sharp knife and set aside until you are ready to start cooking. You only want to cook the cabbage for the briefest moment so leave it until you are just about ready to serve. In a saucepan, add the butter and a splash of water and place on a high heat. When the butter has melted, add the cabbage and the seasoning and mix the cabbage with a spoon until it has softened and is well coated with the butter. Place the cabbage into a colander to strain off any excess liquid.

For the bread

1 loaf of unsliced sandwich bread
softened butter

Preheat your oven to 160°C (315°F/Gas 2–3). I am using a buttered croûte for this recipe; if you want to use a burger bun then that will be very nice as well. Another option (if you can be bothered) is to use the pitta bread recipe on page 115 and shape little buns from that. Otherwise, take the loaf and cut into 12 slices then, using a round cutter, cut rings from the bread that are roughly the same size or bigger than your patties. Brush each side of the bread with softened butter and bake for about 8 minutes, or until golden and toasted.

For serving

vegetable oil

In a large ovenproof frying pan, heat a little oil and cook the crépinette until brown on one side, then flip over and cook for another couple of minutes. Add all of the reserved sauce from the beef cheeks, then place the pan into your oven for 10–12 minutes. Your crépinettes are ready when they are golden and the sauce they are sitting in is well reduced and rich.

Place one piece of the croûte down, then some drained cabbage, beetroot and finish with one of the crépinettes and a good drizzle of the sauce before topping with another croûte. Repeat to make six burgers. I like to serve these with fries (page 138).

I was racking my brain for ages about different ways to do a burger at the café. It has always been met with sighs from my chefs, 'Not a burger!', and so I have been reluctant to do it as I truly think that if you can stimulate a cook's interest the end result will always be much better. But if you cook something you don't like, well, the result will be okay but far from fantastic. So one night I declared that we do a dish called '*Crépinette de joue de boeuf braise au vin rouge en millefeuille de legumes d'viver, croutons d'or et parfum de truffles*' (excuse my French). Penny, my head chef, who is pretty well-versed in kitchen French, rolled her eyes and muttered under her breath, 'I'll let him get it out of his system' but everyone else was curious and interested. The end result was a beef burger. Even though it was a little fancy and not what you would get from just any old burger joint, it was a beef burger nonetheless. This recipe does require a little bit of planning as your butcher will probably have to order in the cheek and the caul fat. Caul is a fine membrane from the stomach of the pig, and has a wonderful ability to hold the filling during the cooking process but, by the end of cooking, it will have almost completely dissolved.

Celeriac and celery salad

for eight to share or four for a light meal

This is a great salad using beautiful raw autumnal vegetables. It's hearty enough to serve on its own as a lunch dish. The salsa verde will make more than you need and will keep for at least 2 weeks in the fridge—try it on grilled meat.

For the celery salsa verde

1 head of celery
½ bunch of flat-leaf (Italian) parsley
1 clove of garlic
8 anchovy fillets
120 g (4¼ oz/¾ cup) salted capers, soaked for
    2 hours, then rinsed and squeezed dry
extra virgin olive oil
salt and ground black pepper

Remove all of the celery leaves from the celery. Now the chopping begins—you can do this in the food processor but you will get a much better result if you use a sharp chopping knife. Finely chop the following: 2 stalks of celery, the celery leaves, parsley, garlic, anchovies and capers.

Combine all of your ingredients in a bowl and stir in enough extra virgin olive oil to form a paste. Taste your salsa verde and adjust the seasoning accordingly but just keep in mind that the salt from the capers and anchovies will develop more as it sits so don't add too much salt.

For serving

1 head of celeriac
1 lemon
a pinch of salt
about 100 g (3½ oz) piece of young pecorino
    cheese (it needs to be soft enough to
    crumble)
4 soft-boiled eggs

To assemble the salad, peel your celeriac and slice about 2 mm (1/16 in) thick, then carefully cut the slices into thin batons, but not too thin. Place the celeriac in a bowl, squeeze over the lemon juice and sprinkle with salt and combine really well, then let this sit for a couple of minutes. Now add half your salsa verde and combine really well. Present the salad on a platter and, to finish, crumble over your pecorino cheese and top with your halved eggs.

As an alternative, this salad can be served warm if you wish—simply blanch the celeriac in boiling salted water for no more than 10–15 seconds so the pieces still retain their crunch and then dress in the salsa verde.

Raw and candied beetroot with goat's cheese

for six to share

I firmly believe that fresh ingredients produced locally are far superior to just about anything. A great example of this was when I received some fantastic beetroots that were delivered to me on the same day as they were picked. They were about the size of my fist and were so juicy they literally bled when I cut into one. I then had a dilemma: do I cook them or do I serve them raw? And being someone who simply hates having to choose, I decided to show them off by serving both raw and candied beetroot.

Raw beetroot is quite dense and hard, but when sliced thinly and served in layers, it allows you to enjoy its sweet, lively flavour. When you cook beetroot, the flavour changes—it becomes more intense, more aromatic and has a delicate yet firm texture. When I cook the candied beetroots I prefer to use an apple liquor from the central ranges in New South Wales made by Orange Mountain Wines (yes, that's right: apple liquor made in Orange) because it is not too alcoholic or rich but has a delicious apple flavour. Using apple cider or another apple liquor will still give you really great results.

Raw and candied beetroot with goat's cheese

pictured page 104

For the preparation of the beetroot

6–8 beetroots (beets) with stalks, about
150–175 g (5½–6 oz) each

Take the whole beetroots and wash well in cold water, including the stems. Cut the stems off at the base and pick through the leaves, choosing the smallest leaves to use as a salad to garnish the final dish. Take about 18 of the best looking stems and slice them as thinly as you can—you will need 10 g (¼ oz/1 cup). Set aside. Peel all the beetroot. Some of these will be cooked and used in the candied beetroot and the others will be sliced and served raw.

For the candied beetroot

a splash of olive oil
4 French shallots, finely diced
10 g (¼ oz/1 cup) thinly sliced beetroot stems
1 small red chilli, split and seeded
salt and ground black pepper
4–5 of your peeled beetroots, diced
300 ml (10½ fl oz) apple liquor or
    alcoholic cider

Heat a saucepan with the oil over medium heat and start by softening the shallot and beetroot stems, then add the chilli and season well. Add the diced beetroot to the pan, then pour in the liquor. Cook for about 30 minutes until the beetroot has become tender and the liquor has almost completely evaporated. What you want to be left with is tender beetroot with a bit of crunch, surrounded in a sweet reduced syrup.

For the sliced raw beetroot

the remainder of your peeled beetroots
a drizzle of peppery extra virgin olive oil
salt and ground black pepper

You want to be able to slice the beetroots as thinly as possible: the easiest way to do this is using a mandolin but you can also use a large sharp knife, taking great care. Arrange the beetroot slices around a platter, then drizzle with oil and season.

For serving

a splash of olive oil
salt and ground black pepper
about 150 g (5½ oz) soft goat's cheese, sliced
a few sprigs of fresh marjoram

In a small bowl, dress the reserved small tender beetroot leaves with a little olive oil, salt and pepper. Arrange the candied beetroots over the raw beetroot slices, scatter with the beetroot leaves and then place pieces of goat's cheese on top. Finish by sprinkling with a little marjoram.

Polenta cake with mushrooms, peas and rocket

for four to share

Polenta is great isn't it? In my last book I harped on about how nice it was to serve soft polenta. Well, this recipe calls for something different—a fried polenta cake. The main thing to remember when cooking this is not to be stingy with how much oil you use; in fact, you want the oil to come at least halfway up the polenta cake. In this recipe I have pan-fried the polenta, but if you have a deep-frier, you can cook the polenta cake that way. Don't worry too much about your polenta cake tasting oily or greasy; it won't be if your oil is at the correct temperature. There are a couple of ways to check the temperature of your oil; the most accurate is with a thermometer but you can also use the handle of a wooden spoon by dipping it in and seeing if bubbles come off it. Or, there is my favourite way—if you take a cube of white bread, drop it into your oil and it takes approximately 45 seconds to go a deep golden brown, then your oil is at 175°C (350°F).

To make a good polenta cake is dead easy. The biggest mistake that people make is to think that just because it needs to set the polenta can't have butter and cheese in it, or that it needs to be extra dry—not so. In fact, all that will happen is that when you re-cook the polenta it will be dry, hard and without flavour. When making your polenta cake it should be as delicious and as wet as you would like to eat your soft polenta.

For preparing the polenta

- 1 litre (35 fl oz/4 cups) water
- 1 bay leaf
- salt and pepper
- 250 g (9 oz/1⅔ cups) polenta
- 125 g (4½ oz/1¼ cups) freshly grated parmesan cheese
- 100 g (3½ oz) diced, cold unsalted butter

Lightly grease a baking tray with a lip so it is ready for when the polenta is cooked. In a large saucepan, combine the water, bay leaf and salt and pepper and bring to a simmer. As soon as the water simmers, slowly start sprinkling in the polenta while continuously stirring with a wooden spoon. When all of the polenta has been added, keep cooking over a very gentle heat for about 20 minutes, stirring from time to time. Taste the polenta to check for doneness—it should have a slightly grainy consistency but should not be 'bitsy'.

When the polenta is ready, remove the pan from the heat, take out the bay leaf and add all of the cheese and butter and stir vigorously until everything is well incorporated. Taste this and adjust the seasoning. Pour the soft polenta into your greased baking tray and, using the back of a spoon, smooth out the polenta. Press on a piece of plastic wrap to cover the polenta and place the tray into your fridge to allow to cool completely—this will take 2–3 hours.

Polenta cake with mushrooms, peas and rocket

pictured page 105

For the mushroom topping

200 g (7 oz) portobello mushrooms, lower part of the stems removed, cut into quarters

200 g (7 oz) button mushrooms, cut in half

150 g (5½ oz) fresh porcini mushrooms, cut into thick slices, or 80 g (2¾ oz) dried porcini, which have been soaked in warm water for 1 hour, then chopped

200 g (7 oz) butter

a few sprigs of thyme

2 cloves of garlic, crushed

salt and ground black pepper

100 g (3½ oz/1 cup) green peas, cooked

a drizzle of extra virgin olive oil

1 lemon

1 large handful of rocket (arugula)

Preheat your oven to 190°C (375°F/Gas 5). Start preparing the mushrooms, then cook the polenta cake while the mushrooms are finishing in the oven. Combine the raw mushrooms and place onto a roasting tray that is large enough to take everything without mounding up high (a relatively thin layer will give the best results). Take your butter and cut into small dice and scatter over the mushrooms along with the sprigs of thyme and the garlic, then season. Put in your oven for about 15 minutes, stir well and return to the oven for another 5–10 minutes. If you are using the dried porcini, then add to the mushrooms about halfway through the cooking.

When the mushrooms are nicely roasted, place them into a bowl with the peas—there should be enough warmth in the mushrooms to warm the peas. Drizzle a little olive oil over the top and squeeze in a touch of lemon juice, then add the rocket and gently fold everything together.

For cooking the polenta cake

vegetable oil

When your polenta has chilled and set, it needs to be cut into pieces and fried. The size of the pieces will depend on the shape and size of your tray. I normally cut them into 4 x 8 cm (1½ x 3¼ in) long batons as they are easy to handle, but use your judgement to get the most out of your tray of polenta.

Heat a large frying pan with about 5 mm (¼ in) of vegetable oil. When the oil is nice and hot, carefully place in the polenta pieces (cook in batches if needed) and cook undisturbed for at least 5 minutes, or until you have a nice golden colour; if you handle the polenta too much, or try moving it before it has coloured properly, then it can break up and crumble. Carefully turn over the polenta and fry the other side. Lift out of the pan and drain on paper towel before transferring to your platter.

For serving

a block of parmesan cheese

Scatter the roasted mushroom mixture over the pieces of polenta, then, using a vegetable peeler, shave over a good amount of parmesan cheese. Serve as soon as you can.

Blue eye cod in clam chowder

for four to share

Clam chowder is 'as American as the Stars and Stripes, as patriotic as the national anthem. It is "Yankee Doodle in a kettle".' So writes Joseph C Lincoln. However, it is believed that the recipe was introduced to the USA by French and English fishermen. Whatever its history or origins, this recipe is a little different from any other I have seen. I wanted to create a chowder that was a meal and had to be shared, and I also wanted to show off the quality of the produce we were using and basically take the recipe up a notch or two. In order to change the chowder I actually used a recipe that I discovered was written in 1751, which makes note of a technique called 'chowder layering ingredients'. It seems that the original chowder was not an 'everything chopped up small' affair at all, but rather ingredients that were layered in different stages in the same dish, cooked and then the final broth thickened with crackers.

When buying the clams ask if they have been purged; if not, when you get home simply cover the clams with cold tap water, add a little salt and leave in your fridge for at least 8–10 hours but no longer than 24 hours.

Blue eye cod in clam chowder

For the croutons

6 slices of stale white bread
3 tablespoons butter, melted

Preheat your oven to 190°C (375°F/Gas 5). Remove the crusts from the bread and cut the bread into small cubes. Place in a bowl, drizzle with butter and mix. Put on a baking tray, then bake for about 5 minutes until golden and crunchy.

For the chowder

120 g (4¼ oz) smoky bacon, chopped
a knob of butter
1 large white onion, peeled and finely diced
1 clove of garlic, chopped
2 tablespoons plain (all-purpose) flour
½ teaspoon smoky paprika
500 ml (17 fl oz/2 cups) milk
300 ml (10½ fl oz) fish stock or water
200 ml (7 fl oz) cream
1 large desiree or other all-purpose potato,
    peeled and cut into dice the size of a pea
1 bunch of thyme
2 bay leaves
a couple of sprigs of marjoram
a couple of sprigs of oregano
ground black pepper
1 piece of blue eye cod, about 800 g (1 lb 12 oz),
    skin removed (avoid the tail piece to ensure
    even cooking)
24 large clams or about 40 vongole (baby
    clams), purged

I like to use a wide flat flameproof casserole dish that will comfortably take all of your ingredients (it needs to have a lid). Place your bacon into the bottom of your cold casserole dish and add a knob of butter, place on a low heat and allow the fat to render out of the bacon, while letting the bacon take on a nice brown colour—this should take about 5 minutes. When you are happy with the colour of the bacon, remove the

meat from the dish, leaving as much of the fat in the dish as possible, then add the onion and garlic. Cook this until the onion is nice and soft, then add the flour and paprika and cook this mixture for another 5 minutes or so.

Add the liquids a little at a time to avoid any lumps forming. When all the liquid has been incorporated, add the diced potato, thyme, bay, marjoram, oregano and a really good grinding of black pepper but hold back on the salt for now as the clams will add their own saltiness. Once you have a gentle simmer, carefully add the cod in one piece, then place the clams around the fish—the fillet should be just covered with liquid, but it doesn't matter if the clams are not completely covered. Cover with the lid.

Move the chowder ingredients about from time to time to make sure that everything is cooking evenly. What will happen is the clams will steam open, releasing their juices and the cooking cod will also be flavouring the soup. You want to take care not to overcook the fish; you actually want to turn off the heat just before the fish is cooked, as it is going to remain in the liquid and will continue to keep cooking. The cooking time depends on the thickness of your fillet: a basic rule of thumb is to cook for 8–12 minutes, then check your fish by pushing with your finger or a spoon. Blue eye cod and other thick flaky white fish will feel almost bouncy just before it is cooked—if you experiment on a raw piece of fish you will know what I mean. Raw fish feels almost hard, nearly cooked will feel bouncy, and overcooked will feel spongy and dry.

For serving

a sprinkle of chopped flat-leaf (Italian) parsley

Serve this chowder at the table with a scattering of parsley and the croutons—you will need to serve it with a ladle and a pair of tongs.

Preserved octopus salad with olives and fennel

for eight to share

This recipe calls for giant octopus, which commonly gets caught in lobster pots in South Australia; it is absolutely delicious. The type of octopus available to you will depend on where you live and what is available at the fishmarkets. Baby octopus is readily available but I prefer not to use it for this recipe. If, however, that is all you can get, cut the octopus into larger pieces, or even just in half, and pay really close attention to how much cooking they receive as they will overcook quite easily. I have given instructions here for how to clean and gut the octopus, but if you can get your fishmonger to do it, even better. It's not that it is a difficult job but it's not much fun.

For the octopus

- 2 kg (4 lb 8 oz) giant octopus
- 1 tablespoon coriander seeds
- 1 teaspoon fennel seeds
- ¼ teaspoon chilli flakes
- ground black pepper
- 1 litre (35 fl oz/4 cups) olive oil (not extra virgin)
- 300 ml (10½ fl oz) dry white wine
- 150 g (5½ oz/about ¾ cup) olives, such as kalamata, ligurian or manzanella
- 4 stalks of celery, finely diced
- ½ head of fennel, finely diced
- 6 cloves of garlic, crushed
- 2 large red chillies, split and seeded
- 1 lemon, peeled, peel reserved
- 4 bay leaves
- lemon juice or white vinegar, optional

Start by cleaning the octopus in plenty of cold water and give it a really good scrub, then remove from the water and pat dry with a clean cloth. Place the octopus onto your chopping board and remove the head by cutting just above the tentacles. Carefully slice up the back of the head, take a firm grip and open the head sac up and remove all the guts, then rinse the head clean. Cut the head in half. Now remove the beak from the middle of the legs and cut the legs into pieces about 10 cm (4 in) long.

Place the octopus pieces in a bowl with the coriander and fennel seeds, chilli flakes and plenty of black pepper.

Choose a large, high-sided saucepan that will comfortably fit all the ingredients—they should only come about halfway up the pan; this will eliminate the chance of any oil boiling over during cooking.

Heat the oil in the pan over a high heat and, when the oil is very hot, very carefully lower in the octopus pieces, taking care not to let the oil boil over. When the octopus is in the pan it will cool the oil down; keep the heat on high and stir the octopus from time to time. As the temperature increases and the moisture is cooked out, the octopus will start to fry again, this can take about 20–30 minutes. You will know it is frying because the oil starts to sound different.

When this happens, carefully add the wine a splash at a time at first to avoid the oil boiling over. When you have added all of the wine, keep cooking on a high heat until almost all of the wine has evaporated. You will be able to tell this because when you first start cooking the wine the oil will look quite milky, but as the wine cooks out, the oil will start to become clear.

Now add the olives, celery, fennel, garlic, chillies, lemon peel and bay leaves and stir really well. Keep the pan on a high temperature and keep cooking until the vegetables and octopus feel tender when tested with the tip of a knife. Depending on the size of the octopus this last stage can take anywhere from 5–30 minutes—when checking the octopus, choose one of the large

pieces. Taste some of the octopus and adjust the seasoning if needed; you can also add a splash of lemon juice or white vinegar to the octopus if you prefer a more 'pickled' flavour.

The octopus is now ready to serve straight away but its flavour is nicer if left for a couple of days in the oil in the fridge. If you do want to keep this longer than a few days, then simply place everything into a sterilized jar (you'll need one that has about a 1.5 litre (52 fl oz/6-cup capacity) and ensure that everything is completely covered with oil—any bits poking out will become mouldy and go off quite quickly. This will keep in the fridge for up to 3 weeks.

For the salad

1 head of fennel
1 lemon
1 handful of flat-leaf (Italian) parsley, coarsely
   chopped

To make the salad, shave the fennel into a bowl, then add a tiny bit of grated lemon zest, the juice from the lemon and the parsley.

For serving

olive oil, optional
salt and ground black pepper

Remove the octopus from the oil, slice as thinly as possible and place in the bowl with the fennel. Use a slotted spoon to collect some of the cooked vegetables from the octopus oil. There should be enough oil on the octopus and the vegetables to dress the salad—but if not simply add a little more. Add a little more salt and pepper and gently toss the salad and serve immediately.

A nice way to roast a leg of lamb

pictured page 113

for eight to share

You'll get the best results for your roast leg of lamb if you have a roasting tin that will just fit the leg of lamb. Most butchers will cut the shank in half, which has always bugged me! Instead, stop him before he does anything silly to your lamb shank and instead ask him to cut under the shank through the back of the leg, but not all the way through so as to avoid cutting into the meat itself (another good reason to buy meat from the butcher and not the supermarket). You will still be able to fold the leg so it will fit into your tin, but the shank will stay lovely and moist and in one piece.

plenty of salt and ground black pepper
1 leg of lamb, leg bone in, but hip bone removed, about 2.5–3 kg (5 lb 8 oz–6 lb 12 oz)
olive oil
1 kg (2 lb 4 oz) baby (pickling) onions, cut in half
2 white onions, thinly sliced
2 cloves of garlic, crushed

Preheat your oven to 190°C (375°F/Gas 5). Season the meat really well. Heat a roasting tin on top of your stove until it is nice and hot, then add a good amount of olive oil and seal and brown your meat really well. Remove the meat from the tin. Add both types of onions to the tin and cook for about 5 minutes until they just start to soften. The baby onions have a good sweet flavour and keep a nice shape, while the thinly sliced white onions are a lot juicier and tend to almost dissolve—this will help your finished sauce to have a good consistency.

When the onions have softened, return the meat to the tin and nestle it among the onions. Cook in your preheated oven for about 1 hour and 15 minutes. During the cooking process, turn the meat a couple of times and, as the onions on top brown, stir back underneath the onions on the bottom. If you feel that the lamb and onions are colouring too quickly, splash a little water into the tin and cover with foil until the end of the cooking time. Remove the lamb from the oven and let the leg rest in the roasting tin for at least 20 minutes before serving.

Roasted lamb leg with pomegranates, avocado and pitta bread

pictured page 117

for eight to share

This is a dish that will benefit greatly from not trying to be too fancy—instead, place all of the components of the dish on the table and let everyone help themselves—it adds real life to the table. Just for fun, put the lamb on the table first with a carving fork and a knife, then walk back into the kitchen while saying, 'Could the alpha male of the table carve the meat', then leave to get the rest of the meal. I like to do this with a new group of people to see who will be the first one to finally crack and start carving up the meat, or to see who will jostle for position and grab the carving knife first. The best example of this was when I recently catered for a group of 150 people. It was a business function with few of the guests knowing each other; at first the mood of the table was fairly stiff and sombre, but 5 minutes after leaving a whole joint of meat on the table and making the announcement it sounded like a real party with everyone talking, laughing and swapping 'meat carving' stories. By the end of the meal everyone declared it was the best meal and the most fun they had ever had at a work function. Fun adds more flavour than salt! You can use pre-made pitta bread; if you are going to make your own pitta I would recommend making the bread before putting together the rest of the recipe as there are a few bits to this recipe. However, don't let this put you off; the salads are straightforward and you should have no problem making everything except the pitta bread in the time it takes to roast the lamb (using the recipe on page 114).

For the pitta bread

1 tablespoon dried yeast
5 tablespoons honey
800 ml (28 fl oz) lukewarm water
1.3 kg (3 lb/10½ cups) plain (all-purpose) flour
a large pinch of salt
oil, for greasing

Put the yeast, honey and water in a bowl and stir to dissolve the yeast; allow this to sit for about 10 minutes. Sift the flour and salt into a large bowl, make a well in the centre and quickly add the water and yeast mixture. Form into a dough and knead for a couple of moments until the dough is soft and just a little sticky. Lightly oil a clean bowl and place the dough into this bowl, cover with a damp cloth and leave to prove for about 2 hours; it should double its size. When you are ready, knock back the dough and divide into 12 equal-sized pieces. Form the pieces into balls, then, using the heel of your hand, flatten them out into flat round loaves about 1 cm (½ in) thick.

Preheat your oven to 250°C (500°F/Gas 9) (or as hot as it will go) and lightly grease two baking trays. Place the pitta breads onto the baking trays and bake for about 4 minutes, then turn over and cook for a further 4 minutes, or until just browned. If you are not serving straight away allow the bread to cool on a wire rack.

For the pomegranate salad

80 g (2¾ oz) French shallots, finely chopped
a pinch of salt
a pinch of sugar
a few grinds of black pepper

continued next page

80 ml (2½ fl oz/⅓ cup) white vinegar
150 ml (5 fl oz) extra virgin olive oil
3 large pomegranates
150 ml (5 fl oz) pomegranate molasses
1 small handful of mixed chopped mint and
    chopped flat-leaf (Italian) parsley

Place the finely chopped shallots into a small bowl and season with the salt, sugar, pepper and vinegar. Leave this to sit for about 20 minutes to allow the shallot to pickle slightly. Whisk in the oil, then check that you are happy with the seasoning.

To prepare the pomegranates, cut the fruit in half and place the cut side of the pomegranate down onto the palm of your hand. Working over a bowl to catch the seeds, whack the tough skin of the pomegranate to shake out all of the seeds. Add the rest of the ingredients to the seeds, stir well and season to taste.

For the toasted couscous and almond salad

120 g (4¼ oz/¾ cup) blanched almonds
100 ml (3½ fl oz) olive oil
1 tablespoon cumin seeds
250 g (9 oz/1⅓ cups) couscous
350 ml (12 fl oz) chicken stock or water, boiling
salt and ground black pepper
¼ bunch of flat-leaf (Italian) parsley, chopped
1 preserved lemon, flesh and pith discarded, skin
    diced as finely as possible
2 tomatoes, finely diced

For this recipe you will need a saucepan with a tight-fitting lid. Place your almonds onto your chopping board and, using the flat of your knife, break into irregular pieces, but try not to crush them into a powder.

Put the oil, cumin and almonds in the saucepan over a high heat and toast until you have a very light brown colour. Add the couscous and continue to toast everything until the couscous has started to turn light brown. Pour in your boiling stock or water in one go,

stir a couple of times and cover with a lid as quickly as you can. Turn off the heat and allow your couscous to sit undisturbed for 10–12 minutes, then remove the lid and, using a fork, fluff up the couscous to remove any lumps; keep working until it is all nice and loose, taste and season accordingly. If you leave the lid on, the couscous will stay warm for about 20 minutes, or you can reheat it in the microwave or serve at room temperature. When you are just about to serve, add the parsley, preserved lemon and tomato and fluff up once more.

For the avocado salad

juice of 1 lime
60 ml (2 fl oz/¼ cup) sesame oil
125 ml (4 fl oz/½ cup) extra virgin
    olive oil
2 large red chillies, seeded and cut into thin strips
salt and ground black pepper
4 ripe avocados
a few leaves of mint
a few leaves of coriander (cilantro)

Make this salad last so it is as fresh as possible. Place the lime juice, oils, chilli, salt and ground black pepper in a bowl and whisk gently. Cut the avocados in half and remove the seeds. Using a large tablespoon, scoop out bite-sized chunks of avocado into irregular shapes and drop them into the bowl of dressing. When all the avocado is in the bowl, add the mint and coriander leaves and fold very gently with your hands. Taste and add more seasoning if it is needed.

For serving

1 roasted lamb leg with onions (page 114), carved

Place your lamb in the middle of the table with bowls of the salads and a stack of your pitta breads. Invite your guests to tear open one end of the pitta to make a pocket and put some of the couscous in first as this will catch all the juices from the other ingredients.

Cape gooseberry clafoutis with gooseberry mascarpone

for eight

A clafoutis is a simple batter cake that benefits from its batter being prepared the day before, as the almonds give off a better flavour if they have been allowed to infuse into the batter. But if you really have a craving and need to make the clafoutis and eat it straight away, then you will still get good results. The real trick to cooking clafoutis is serving it straight out of the oven while it is light and puffy.

For the batter

100 g (3½ oz/⅔ cup) almonds, lightly toasted
25 g (1 oz/¼ cup) plain (all-purpose) flour
a pinch of salt
200 g (7 oz/scant 1 cup) caster (superfine) sugar
4 eggs and 6 yolks, lightly beaten together
250 ml (9 fl oz/1 cup) pouring (whipping) cream

Grind the almonds in a food processor until ground but with a few large bits remaining. Tip into a bowl. Place the flour and salt into the food processor and pulse a few times, then add the sugar and blend for a brief moment, then add the almonds and return to the processor and give another brief blend. While the blender is running, add the eggs and cream. Only blend for as long as it takes for everything to combine. Pour into a container and cover with plastic wrap, then place this in your fridge overnight.

For the gooseberry mascarpone

100 g (3½ oz) cape gooseberries (physalis),
    removed from their husks
55 g (2 oz/¼ cup) sugar
a splash of lemon juice
200 g (7 oz/scant 1 cup) mascarpone
45–80 ml (1½–2½ fl oz) pouring (whipping)
    cream

Put your gooseberries, sugar and lemon juice in a bowl and, using the back of a wooden spoon, smash and crush the gooseberries into a really chunky pulp.

Let this sit at room temperature for about 1 hour, then add the mascarpone and a splash of the cream and use your wooden spoon to combine everything together, only adding as much cream as you need to combine everything into a soft cream that just holds its shape.

To cook the clafoutis

some butter, at room temperature
some caster (superfine) sugar
400 g (14 oz) cape gooseberries (physalis)

You can make individual clafoutis using eight dishes about 14 cm (5½ in) across and 1.5 cm (⅝ in) deep. Alternatively, make one large clafoutis in a dish about 25 cm (10 in) across and 2 cm (¾ in) deep.

Take some of the butter in your fingers and smear it all over the surface of the dish(es), then spoon in the sugar and shake the dish(es) to completely coat the butter with sugar, then shake out any excess. Scatter in the gooseberries, then stir your batter really well before pouring it in.

Clafoutis is best cooked in a fan-forced oven. If your oven is not fan-forced, increase the temperature by 10°C (20°F). Cook individual clafoutis in a preheated 210°C (415°F/Gas 6–7) oven for about 12 minutes. For a large clafoutis, cook in a preheated 190°C (375°F/Gas 5) oven for 24 minutes. The clafoutis is ready when it is just set in the middle and golden and brown around the edges, and it should also puff up almost like a soufflé. Take straight to the table and serve with a dollop of the gooseberry mascarpone.

How to cook quinces

I use this method to cook quinces for both the orange and quince cake (page 122), as well as using the syrup in a quince royale (page 90). This is a great recipe because once your quinces are prepared and cooked they will last for a few months in the fridge.

2 kg (4 lb 8 oz) quinces
1 kg (2 lb 4 oz/4½ cups) sugar
2 litres (70 fl oz/8 cups) water
2 cinnamon sticks
zest and juice of 1 lemon
zest of 1 orange
4 cloves
2 bay leaves
500 ml (17 fl oz/2 cups) red wine
10 black peppercorns

Quinces are very hard, which makes them difficult to cut so it is important to use a sharp knife and be very careful. Start by peeling the quinces using a sharp vegetable peeler, then carefully cut the quinces into quarters and remove the cores. Reserve all of the peeling and cores and place them onto a large piece of muslin (cheesecloth) or a clean tea towel (dish towel), then roll up into a parcel and tie up securely with twine.

Preheat your oven to 180°C (350°F/Gas 4). Choose a large saucepan that will be able to go into a hot oven. Prepare your cooking liquid by combining the remaining ingredients in the saucepan and bring it up to the boil. Carefully add the prepared quinces, then add the parcel of cores and seeds to help keep your quinces under the liquid. Bring this up to a simmer and then place into the oven for anywhere from 3–5 hours. What you will notice is that as they are cooking, the quince will start off pale and hard, then it will turn pale and very soft—during this stage do not stir the fruit or it will break up. About halfway through cooking it will start to become pink, then, as it cooks further it will start to deepen in colour to burgundy red and the flesh will start to firm up slightly. When you are at this stage, remove the quinces from the oven and allow to cool completely in the liquid. Remove the fruit and place

into a large jar or container. Place the liquid back on the heat and bring to the boil, reduce the liquid by a third, then remove from the heat and allow to cool. When the syrup is completely cold, strain it back over the fruit. The fruit should be completely covered by the liquid, and this will preserve the fruit for a few months in the fridge.

Quinces with cream and amaretti biscuit
for four

4 nice pieces of cooked quince with their syrup
about 200 g (7 oz) clotted cream
about 8 amaretti biscuits (cookies)

Simply place a piece of the quince into a dessert bowl and place a blob of cream next to it. Now pour over a little of the syrup before finally crumbling an amaretti biscuit over the top.

Orange and quince cake

for ten

This is a moist cake that can easily last for up to 2 days. This means that when you have people over and you want to dish them up something special but easy, and you want to make sure that there are enough leftovers for a tasty morning tea for yourself the next day, then this is the cake for you. If you take time to boil the oranges correctly you will get a truly fantastic result. The other main component of this recipe is the quinces—you can substitute these for almost any other fruit, or even leave the fruit out of it altogether and have a simple orange cake.

2 oranges
250 g (9 oz/heaped 1 cup) caster (superfine)
    sugar
6 eggs
250 g (9 oz/2½ cups) ground almonds
1½ teaspoons baking powder
unsalted butter, for greasing
plain (all-purpose) flour, for dusting
8–10 cooked quince pieces (page 120)

Preheat your oven to 150°C (300°F/Gas 2). Start by placing the whole oranges into a saucepan and cover with cold water. Place onto a high heat and bring the water to a boil. As soon as it boils, strain off the water and cover with fresh cold water and then return to the heat until it boils again. Repeat this process six times, each time exchanging the boiled water for fresh cold water. What this process achieves is to gently coax the bitter, harsh flavours out of the orange skin while cooking the oranges until they are soft enough to purée. After you have tipped off the final batch of water, allow the oranges to cool enough to handle before cutting into quarters and carefully removing any seeds. Place the oranges (peel and all) into a food processor and blend really well. While the oranges are blending, add the sugar and eggs and blend some more, then add the ground almonds and baking powder and give it one more blend.

Take a 24 cm (9½ in) spring-form tin and rub with a little butter, then add a big pinch of flour to the tin and shake the flour around until the entire surface of the tin has been coated. Arrange pieces of quince over the bottom of the tin, then pour in the orange mixture. Bake for about 1 hour. Your cake is cooked when you insert a skewer and it comes out clean.

Sour cherry and apple parfait with a negroni chaser

for eight

This is a good frozen dessert that is almost like ice cream without the effort of churning. This dessert reminds me of a 'spider', which is something we used to have as a treat when we were kids (take a glass of cola and add a scoop of ice cream), so when I sit down to this dessert it seems like a lot of fun. I like to use the negroni in this dessert as it gives a delicious bitter flavour that works well with the cherries and apple. As the cocktail is strong and bitter I normally serve it on the side and let people add it to the parfait as they wish.

For the parfait

150 ml (5 fl oz) dry white wine
80 g (2¾ oz/⅓ cup) caster (superfine) sugar
4 golden delicious apples, peeled, cored and quartered
1 cinnamon stick
1 tablespoon Calvados
50 g (1¾ oz) sour cherries or dried cranberries
3 egg yolks
extra 80 g (2¾ oz/⅓ cup) caster (superfine) sugar
150 ml (5 fl oz) cream

Place the wine and sugar in a saucepan and warm to dissolve the sugar, then add your apple and cinnamon, cover with a lid and cook gently until the apple is soft. Remove the cinnamon, transfer to a food processor and blend until completely smooth. While you are blending, add the Calvados. Place the apple purée into a bowl, then add the sour cherries.

Place the yolks and the extra sugar into a bowl and whisk until thick, pale and creamy. Place your cream into a third large bowl and whisk until you have soft peaks. Fold the egg yolks, then the apple into the cream.

Pour this mixture into one large container to freeze for at least 6 hours or overnight. Remember to pull it out of the freezer about 20 minutes before you want to serve to allow it to soften a little.

For serving

a few amaretti biscuits (cookies)
4 negroni cocktails (page 89)

Scoop your parfait into individual bowls or glasses, then crumble over the amaretti biscuit. Serve your negroni cocktail in a little glass on the side and encourage everyone to pour a little over the top.

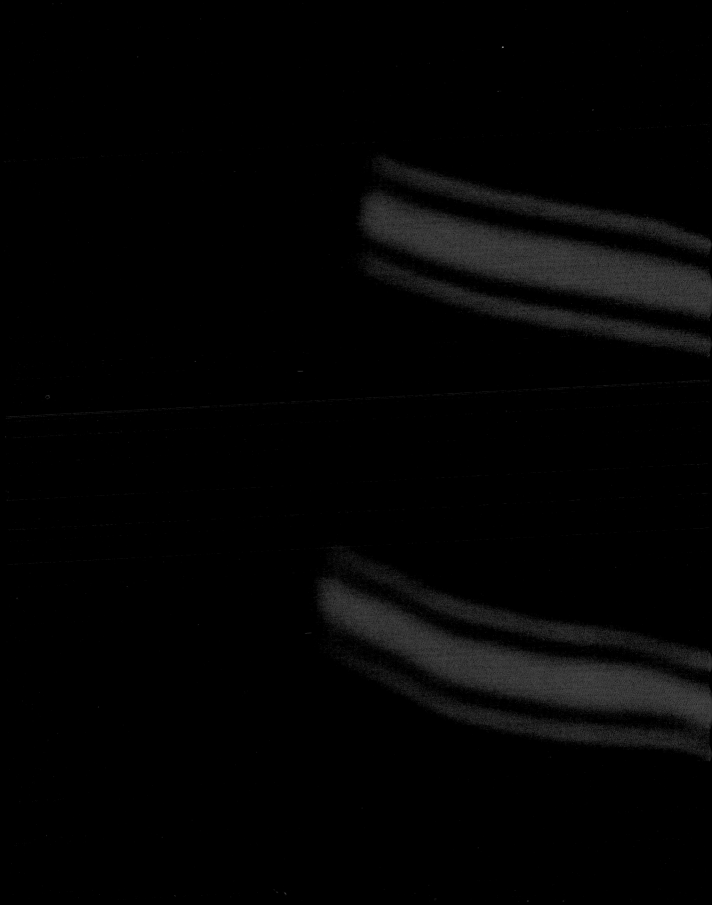

Winter menu
for a shared table

Mulled wine

for six

Like many food traditions, mulled wine was developed out of necessity, which in this case was the need to reuse bad or off wine. The theory was that if you added enough honey and spice to the wine, then you could drink it. But over time, mulled wine has become steeped in tradition as a Christmas drink. In Australia it would be a bit of a punishment to drink mulled wine in the summer heat of a southern hemisphere Christmas, so let's just call it a great winter warmer. There are thousands of variations to mulled wine but I particularly love the rich, warming flavours of the version here.

125 ml (4 fl oz/½ cup) brandy
150 g (5½ oz/⅔ cup) caster (superfine) sugar
100 g (3½ oz) sour cherries
750 ml (26 fl oz/3 cups) red wine (don't waste anything fancy)
2 cinnamon sticks
a pinch of grated nutmeg
3–4 cloves
2 oranges, unpeeled, sliced
1 lemon, unpeeled, sliced
125 ml (4 fl oz/½ cup) weak tea

Start by placing the brandy, sugar and sour cherries in a small saucepan, place over a very gentle heat and gradually warm while stirring to dissolve the sugar. Then add the wine, spices, orange, lemon and tea and return to a very gentle heat, stirring from time to time to allow everything to warm together. Keep it on the heat until it is just about to boil, then strain into heatproof glasses and decorate with a slice of the orange.

Lambs' wool

for ten

This is a great warming drink for those cold winter nights. In England it is traditionally served on November 1 to mark All Saints' Day.

6 green apples
2 litres (70 fl oz/8 cups) good English ale
2 tablespoons raisins
1/2 teaspoon ground nutmeg
1/2 teaspoon ground ginger
120 g (4 1/4 oz/heaped 1/2 cup) sugar

Preheat your oven to 180°C (350°F/Gas 4). Place your apples onto a baking tray and put them in the oven and bake for 10–15 minutes, or until the apples are soft to touch (think just of a baked potato)— if they burst, don't panic because you'll be making an apple purée. Remove them from the oven and, when cool enough to handle, peel, cut in half and remove the core. Now place them into a bowl and mash really well with a potato masher. The apple purée can be made well in advance and kept in the fridge until needed.

Put the apple purée, ale, raisins, spices and sugar in a saucepan and warm, being careful not to allow the mixture to boil. Pour into warmed glasses or mugs.

A white cosmopolitan with burnt orange

for one

My manager, Oliver, showed me the trick I use here, which is to burn a piece of orange peel so the aromatic burnt citrus oil coats the surface of the cocktail, imparting a wonderful aroma and delicious flavour to the drink. The tricky part is burning the orange oil before it is added to the drink. To start, you need to peel off a strip of orange peel—the easiest way to do this is to use a vegetable peeler. To best understand how the orange works in the drink, hold a piece of the orange peel up to the light, fold it in half and give it a good squeeze; you should see the beautiful aromatic oil squirt out of the skin—this is the precious stuff you want in the drink. To burn the orange oil, take your piece of orange peel in one hand and in the other a cigarette lighter. Light the flame and then squeeze the orange peel, so that the oil shoots through the flames onto the surface of the cocktail. This may seem a little like patting your head while rubbing your stomach but it is pretty easy once you get the hang of it.

30 ml (1 fl oz) vodka
15 ml (½ fl oz) Cointreau
15 ml (½ fl oz) white cranberry juice
a splash of lime juice
ice
a piece of orange peel without any pith

Combine all the liquids in a cocktail shaker with plenty of ice, then use a long spoon to stir all of the ingredients really well. Strain into a chilled martini glass. Now burn the orange oil using a cigarette lighter (and following the instructions in the introduction), but do it close enough so that the oil shoots through the flame and lands on the surface of the finished drink. Drop the piece of orange peel into the drink.

Dank and dirty

for one

There is much more to Jägermeister than drunken visits to the snow, though I never believed it until the day when I stopped and actually tasted the stuff. Sure it is strong and herbaceous and not everyone's cup of tea, but have you ever tried it with crushed orange? Absolutely delicious.

The Jägermeister label on the bottle is a reference to Saint Hubertus who was fabled for his purity. One day while out hunting he saw a stag that had a crucifix floating between its antlers. This vision so moved Hubertus that he sold all of his worldly goods and founded several monasteries. After his death he was made a saint and became the patron saint of hunters.

¼ of a blood orange, unpeeled, cut into chunks
90 ml (3 fl oz) Jägermeister
crushed ice

In a cocktail shaker or heavy-bottomed glass, use a stick to muddle the orange and the Jägermeister together, then add a little crushed ice, stir well and pour everything into a glass to serve.

Danks Street Depot's really good nuts

snacks for a few

The name says it all really—this is a recipe that was preceded by loads of failures until I got it perfect. I hope that I have taken out a lot of the hard work for you with this selection of nuts and spices. The nuts should be spicy, but not hot; sweet and salty, but not too much so; and, most of all, they should be crispy. One of the other great pleasures of this recipe is that if you crumble the cinnamon into pieces, it will cook in with the nuts and will be sweet and crispy, which means that every now and then you get this beautiful cinnamon burst.

500 ml (17 fl oz/2 cups) water
500 g (1 lb 2 oz/2¼ cups) sugar
3 cinnamon sticks
4 star anise
1½ teaspoons chilli flakes
55 g (2 oz/¼ cup) salt
200 g (7 oz/2 cups) walnuts
100 g (3½ oz/⅔ cup) almonds
100 g (3½ oz/scant ⅔ cup) macadamia nuts
100 g (3½ oz/⅔ cup) cashew nuts
100 g (3½ oz/⅔ cup) hazelnuts
100 g (3½ oz/⅔ cup) pistachio nuts
100 g (3½ oz/⅔ cup) peanuts
2 litres (70 fl oz/8 cups) oil
chilli powder, for seasoning
salt, for seasoning

You need to have a large heavy-based saucepan to get the best results, but I have also had success in a non-stick electric frying pan with a high lip.

Put the water, sugar, cinnamon, star anise, chilli flakes and salt in your saucepan and bring to the boil. Add all the nuts. Bring to the boil once again, then thoroughly strain the syrup from the nuts and allow to cool for about 30 minutes. (If you have the time you can let the nuts soak in the syrup overnight before straining, which will produce a better flavour.) The nuts must be quite dry before being fried or the oil will splatter dramatically.

Half-fill a large, clean heavy-based saucepan with the oil and heat until it reaches about 170°C (325°F), or until the handle of the wooden spoon dipped in the oil starts to bubble. Carefully lower the nuts, in batches, into the oil and deep-fry each batch for 5–10 minutes until the nuts are a deep golden brown colour, stirring continuously the whole time.

When the nuts are nice and brown, remove them from the oil and place onto a clean dry tea towel (dish towel) over a tray to drain off the excess oil. As the nuts are cooling, stir them from time to time to stop them from clumping together. Allow to cool completely, then season with chilli powder and extra salt.

Welsh rabbit (rarebit)

for four as a nibble

Now I don't want to spark controversy as I am sure that there has been many a pub brawl over this very subject, but it has always been a matter of curiosity to me how a dish that is so steeped in history can have such a weird name that doesn't really seem to have anything to do with any of the primary ingredients. What I have discovered is that recipes dating back to early 1700 called the dish Welsh 'rabbit' and it wasn't until around 1780 or so that recipes started appearing called Welsh 'rarebit'. According to the Wikipedia encyclopedia, 'In 17th and 18th century England it was common to use the term Welsh to mean inferior quality or even counterfeiting'. There are also recipes for English rarebit that use red wine and brown bread and Scotch rarebit that use bread and cheese toasted separately and then put together at the last minute. So the theory is that it is either a derogatory way of saying 'this is not rabbit' or it is a poor copy of the English or Scotch rarebit. All this for cheese on toast!

In this version I have opted for my own variation because it brings back great childhood memories of when I used to sneak cheese by slicing it onto a plate and melting it in the microwave oven and then using toast to scrape it up.

One final word, the better the cheddar the better the result. I prefer Quickes, 24-month clothbound cheddar from Devon in England, but you can still get good results with whatever you have on hand.

a knob of butter
250 g (9 oz) aged cheddar cheese, thinly sliced
2 tablespoons wholegrain mustard
2 teaspoons hot English mustard
80 ml (2½ fl oz/⅓ cup) good English ale
as many thick slices of warm buttered toast as you want

Preheat your oven to 180°C (350°F/Gas 4). Rub a little butter on the bottom of an ovenproof dish that is about 15 cm (6 in) round and 5 cm (2 in) high. Place down a layer of thinly sliced cheddar. Combine the two mustards together and spread a thin layer over the cheese and then splash in some of your ale. Repeat this process until everything has been used up. Place the dish into the oven and cook until the cheese has melted and bubbles slightly around the edges. Serve straight away as a dip with plenty of hot toast and a glass of ale.

Fried truffled egg with green onion soubise
for four to share

I have been lucky enough to finally get hold of some truffles grown in Tasmania. The real joy of this from an Australian perspective is being able to enjoy a beautiful fragrant truffle in winter as opposed to our summer when the French and Italian truffles are in season.

I am always amused by truffles; when you look at them they are jet black, lumpy-looking growths that smell like a gas leak—the amusing part is that someone was game enough to cook with them in the first place. I have this whole routine worked out in my mind where a peasant in a beret is holding up a forkful of potato with a little sliver of truffle, saying to his mate in a thick French accent, 'Non, reeley, taste eet, eet eez amaz-ing'. Even if that is not how it started I think we are all indebted to him and his efforts.

When using truffles, a little bit of forethought goes a long way. I have all the dishes I want to do planned out well in advance of the truffle arriving in the kitchen. The reason for this is that if I want to do a risotto I will have jars half-filled with arborio rice waiting to receive the truffle—once a few truffles are embedded in the rice I top the jar up and seal them. This will allow the rice to absorb the perfume of the truffle itself. The same can also be done with eggs, as an egg shell is porous and will easily absorb the truffle aroma. To do this successfully you must use the freshest eggs you can as it is best to let the eggs and truffle sit together for a couple of days before cooking. You will end up with an egg scented with truffle and then you can use the truffle for cooking.

4 eggs
1 fresh truffle, about 50 g (1¾ oz)
1 bunch of spring onions (scallions)
a knob of butter
salt and ground black pepper
100 ml (3½ fl oz) dry white wine
300 ml (10½ fl oz) cream
oil, for frying
4 thick pieces of sourdough toast

A couple of days in advance, line an airtight jar with tissue paper, carefully add your eggs, then add the truffle. Seal the jar and store in the fridge for 2 days.

To make the soubise, start by preparing your onions: remove the white part of the onion from the green. Slice the white part of the onion thinly and place to one side. Now slice the green part of the onion as thinly as you can and again keep separate.

Melt a little of your butter in a small saucepan but do not let it colour. Add the white part of the spring onion, season with salt and pepper and cook for a few minutes, or until the onion has become very soft. Pour in the wine and cook until it has all but evaporated. Add the cream, bring up to a gentle simmer and cook for 1–2 minutes. Remove from the heat and transfer to a blender and process until it has become smooth. Return to the pan to the heat; once this has started to simmer again, add the green part of the onion and stir well.

While this is all going on you want to heat a large heavy-based frying pan with about 1 cm (½ in) of oil. Carefully crack your eggs into the hot oil; take care doing this as the eggs can spit a little. Once all of the eggs are in the oil, take a spoon and spoon some of the hot oil over the yolks and top of the egg. The perfect fried egg has crispy and fluffy egg whites while the yolk is still runny. Carefully lift your eggs out of the oil and drain briefly on some paper towel.

Place the toast on your plate and spoon over plenty of the soubise, top with an egg, then shave over the truffle using either a truffle slicer or a mandolin.

Pork hock knuckle with chestnuts and onions

for four to six to share

Every year, chestnuts are eyed with suspicion. Most people (in Australia, at least) have heard that they are delicious but don't know what to do with them. They usually end up in desserts but they are just as well suited to meats such as pork and duck. I first discovered cooking chestnuts with onions in an old Jewish cookbook a couple of years back; the irony comes from the fact it is an absolutely delicious combination when cooked with pork! Chestnuts are a little labour intensive but once you get into them they are really not too much of a problem. I also find that the chestnuts available at the beginning of the season tend to be a little smaller and also a little more difficult to peel—in the middle of winter they are larger and easier to deal with.

400 g (14 oz) whole chestnuts
4 onions
2 cloves of garlic
vegetable oil, for frying, plus extra, to rub the
    pork knuckle
a pinch of salt
a few sprigs of thyme
800 ml (28 fl oz) chicken stock or water
2 x 1.3 kg (3 lb) pork knuckle or pork hock,
    with the skin removed
salt and ground black pepper

Preheat your oven to 180°C (350°F/Gas 4). Make a cut that runs lengthways on the rounded side of each chestnut; don't cut too deep, but you do need to cut slightly into the flesh. Roast the chestnuts for about 15 minutes, or until you can see that the skin of the chestnut has peeled back and opened up, revealing little smiles. Remove from the oven and wrap in a clean tea towel (dish towel) until they are cool enough to handle, but keep in mind that they are a lot easier to peel when they are warm. Using a small knife, peel away the tough outer shell and also the skin and, using your hands, break into smallish chunks. Increase the oven temperature to 220°C (425°F/Gas 7).

Thinly slice the onions and garlic. Heat a saucepan with a little vegetable oil and sauté the onions and garlic with a little salt until soft. Add the chestnuts and thyme and cover with chicken stock. Bring to the

boil, then turn down the heat to a simmer. Cover with a tight-fitting lid and cook for about 15 minutes, or until the onions have become very soft and you have a wet saucy consistency. Set aside until needed.

While this is happening, rub the pork hock with a little oil and season generously. Place the pork into a hot, oiled roasting tin and cook on top of your stove until you have coloured the pork all over. Transfer the tin to the oven for 1 hour 40 minutes, being sure to turn your meat every so often to ensure you will get a good even colour on the meat.

Take your roasting tin from the oven, tip off any excess fat and pour in the onion and chestnut mixture. Cover with foil and return to the oven. You will need to cook this for at least another 50 minutes, but be sure to turn your meat every 10–15 minutes and coat with the onion in the tin, as you want to get a nice even brown colour both on the meat and onion. If during the cooking process you feel that the tin is getting dry, or the meat or onions are colouring too quickly, you can control this by adding a splash of stock or water. Cook until the pork is very soft and almost falling off the bone.

I like to serve this by placing the hock in the middle of the table surrounded by the caramelized onion and chestnuts. It's great served with creamy mashed potato or even soft polenta, and a glass of chilled aromatic Gewürztraminer.

How to cook the perfect fries

for a group to share

To cook perfect fries you will need all of the normal utensils, such as a large heavy-based saucepan, a slotted spoon or 'spider' to lift the fries out of the oil and a tray with plenty of paper for draining the fries. Another important piece of equipment is a thermometer (it needs to be a candy or deep-frying thermometer) as it is the most accurate way to test the oil, but if you don't have one I will give you a tip. If you take a small cube of plain bread and drop it into oil that is 175°C (350°F) it will take about 45 seconds for it to go golden brown.

About the potato. A large baking potato such as sebago is my favourite; you can get away with a good all-rounder potato, such as desiree, but avoid anything too waxy or wet, such as kipfler (fingerling) or nicola. You want to cut your fry no thicker than 1 cm (½ in). If you are doing a large quantity put the cut fries in water to stop them from discolouring, but if you are only doing a small batch, then cut them as you place them into the oil for the first frying.

About the oil. I prefer the neutral flavour of cottonseed oil or vegetable oil but beef dripping or duck fat make a wonderful substitute for those who enjoy a more robust flavour. The oil needs to have a high enough smoking point for you to be able to cook without it smoking and giving off an acrid flavour—extra virgin olive oil, for example, is not a good choice as it will start to smoke at a low temperature and its flavour will overpower the potato. The oil will be used twice—one of the secrets to great fries is that you need to cook the potato twice.

About the salt. When you eat a fry, you are eating potato and salt and that's about it. Sounds pretty obvious but it often gets overlooked. So this might be a good time to give you a lesson about salt. First of all, salt is salt. All salt has exactly the same chemical make up—what distinguishes the different types is how and where the salt was refined. The shape and size of salt are important and it's important to know the different options so you choose the right type to match the food you are seasoning. Try the following experiment. Take three pieces of a raw vegetable, such as a tomato or celery. Using about the same quantity of salt, season the first with normal fine ground table salt, the second with a few lumps of rock salt and the third with salt flakes. When you eat the vegetables you will notice that the table salt will taste immediately saltier as the salt easily dissolves straight away and your taste buds get a big salt hit all in one go. Now try the large rock salt—you will get the flavour of unsalted vegetable and then little salt bursts, which give a 'tasty' effect as your taste buds get crunchy little salt bursts. The salt flakes tend to be a good compromise as they will dissolve slightly and give you little salt bursts. But when it comes to fries, you'll find that if you use large rock salt or even salt flakes, the salt will simply fall off and do nothing to the potato. So, in short, salt flakes have a nice aesthetic quality but to season your fries correctly you should use a fine powdered table salt.

oil, for deep-frying
about 1 large potato per person
table salt or celeriac salt (page 14), for sprinkling

Take a large saucepan and fill it no higher than one-third full of oil.

Using a large chopping knife, cut your potatoes no thicker than 1 cm (½ in) and soak them in cold water. This will keep them from browning and will rinse off some of the starch. Remove your potatoes from the water and pat dry—this is very important as you do not want to throw water into your pan of hot oil.

Heat your oil to 140°C (275°F) and start to blanch your fries. Do not overcrowd your pan as you will make the temperature of the oil drop and your fries will not cook correctly. After 3 minutes of cooking, carefully lift out your fries and drain on paper towel. This stage can be done in advance, in fact even 1 day before; of course they are better when you cook them straight away.

When you are ready to serve your fries, bring your oil up to 175°C (350°F) and carefully lower in your fries in batches and cook for 3–4 minutes, or until golden and crispy. Be careful not to overcook the fries as they really are at their best when crunchy on the outside and fluffy in the middle. Drain on paper towel and sprinkle with salt.

Chip butty
for one

There are two types of people in this world. There are those who know what a chip butty is and laugh at the idea that you need to have a recipe for it, and there are those who have never heard of a chip butty and will read this recipe and be a little amused and/or disgusted at the idea of eating it. I usually allow 2 thick slices of bread per person.

piping hot fries (page 138)
2 thick slices of white sandwich loaf bread
a slathering of good salted butter
a dollop of good tomato sauce (ketchup)

Drain the freshly cooked fries on paper towel, then start buttering your bread.

Place your fries onto one side of your bread and now pour in as much tomato sauce as you want. Top with the other piece of bread and press down until melted butter and tomato sauce start to ooze out the sides. Pick up your sandwich with both hands and devour! One piece of advice is that it is best not to watch someone eat a chip butty too closely as it is not a pretty sight.

Fennel and celeriac served with a toasted almond and bacon fat dressing

for eight to share

The idea of cooking in fat might not be to everyone's liking, but it does taste delicious. When I first put this dish on the menu I was a little afraid that it was not going to sell, and that it would scare people off but, no, it was very well received. The reason I like to use back fat here is that it gives an almost creamy finish to the dressing, and the bold clean flavours of the root vegetables respond really well to this. If you have trouble getting hold of pork back fat you can substitute duck fat.

1 large head of celeriac (about 500 g/
    1 lb 2 oz), cut into 8 wedges
1 star anise
salt and ground black pepper
2 large heads of fennel, cut into quarters
a knob of butter
250 g (9 oz) piece of back fat, diced fairly small
100 g (3½ oz/⅔ cup) blanched almonds,
    roughly broken with the flat of your knife
1 clove of garlic, crushed
a little chopped thyme and chopped
    flat-leaf (Italian) parsley
a splash of white wine vinegar

Preheat your oven to 120°C (235°F/Gas ½). Put the celeriac wedges in a saucepan and cover with cold water. Add the star anise, salt and black pepper and bring to a gentle simmer. Now add your fennel. Cook the vegetables for 8–10 minutes, or until tender, then drain and gently toss with a knob of butter and a little more ground black pepper. Transfer the vegetables to a large casserole dish and put into a warm oven.

To make the dressing, put the diced fat in a small frying pan and start to fry over a medium heat, stirring from time to time. You will not need to add any oil as the fat will start to render. When the edges just start to brown, add the almonds, turn the heat up to high and fry everything together until well browned. When you have a delicious nutty aroma and a good brown colour, remove your pan from the heat and add the garlic clove and leave to cook in the heat of the pan. After a moment, add your herbs, vinegar and salt and pepper to taste—you want a good balance of sharpness for a well-flavoured dressing.

Remove your vegetables from the oven (they should have dried slightly by now), scoop into serving dishes and spoon the dressing over the top.

Raw beef with parmesan and onion

for four to share

This recipe was first shown to me by Tony Pappas when I worked at the Bayswater Brasserie and I have included it because it was the first dish I ate that really encompasses the idea of quality products done simply. The success of this dish relies on only four ingredients: beef, onion, parmesan and olive oil. Try skimping on any one of these and it will be to the detriment of the whole dish—so absolutely do not use frozen beef or pre-grated parmesan. You really need a sharp knife to get thin slices of beef, but don't worry too much as I will explain how to achieve the same results regardless.

You need to use a nice piece of aged beef. I find sirloin to be the best for flavour and texture. A nice light amount of fat flaked throughout the meat (called marbling) is important; however, my preference is for something that is not too marbled as it can be a little too rich.

½ small onion
140 g (5 oz) piece of parmesan cheese
salt and ground black pepper
60 ml (2 fl oz/¼ cup) extra virgin olive oil, plus
    a little extra for drizzling
350 g (12 oz) aged sirloin, trimmed

Start by preparing the onion and parmesan. Peel and finely dice the onion, then chop the onion even more on your chopping board to ensure that it is very fine—scrape this into a bowl and add a little salt and black pepper. Now grate your parmesan on the finest side of your grater and add this to your onion. Pour in the olive oil and mix until you have a thick, almost dry paste and season with some more salt and pepper.

Select the platter you wish to serve the beef on, then prepare to slice the beef. If you are a well-trained and accomplished sushi chef you will still have problems getting the beef absolutely perfect so don't panic if you find this a little difficult. You need to slice the beef as thinly as you possibly can, which is easier with an electric slicer or a sharp carving knife. But if your slices aren't as accurate and thin as you'd like, then use the following technique. On your chopping board place a large piece of plastic wrap, now lay down your piece of beef and then place on another large piece of plastic wrap. Using a rubber mallet or the flat of your chopping knife, pound out the meat until it is nice and thin, then lift off your top piece of plastic and lay the meat out on your platter. Repeat the process until all of the meat has been used up.

Once you have arranged the beef, serve it as soon as possible as you don't want to have the meat dry out and lose its flavour. Drizzle over a little more extra oil, then season well with salt and pepper. Place a big dollop of the parmesan and onion over each strip of beef. This is really nice with a little rocket (arugula) salad on the side and some very fresh sourdough bread.

Witlof salad with walnuts

for four to six to share

This is one of those salads that is great to eat in the cooler months as it stands up well against big flavours. I like to serve it with meals such as poached tongue or even fried quail and barbecued meat. I included a similar salad made from radicchio in my last book—I will always include one of them on the menu at the café, depending on whether witlof or radicchio is best at the time.

1 tablespoon white wine vinegar
2 tablespoons honey
90 g (3¼ oz/⅓ cup) wholegrain mustard
1 teaspoon dijon mustard
45 ml (1½ fl oz) extra virgin olive oil
a drizzle of walnut oil (if you have any)
salt and ground black pepper
6 large heads of witlof (chicory/Belgian endive)
125 g (4½ oz/1¼ cups) walnuts, toasted
1 bunch of chives, finely snipped
about 50 g (1¾ oz/½ cup) freshly grated
    parmesan cheese

Start by making your dressing in a small bowl by whisking the vinegar into the honey, then adding both mustards. Finish by adding the oils, salt and pepper.

Take the witlof heads and remove any discoloured outer leaves. Cut lengthways in half and then place the halves, cut side down, on your chopping board. Shred the witlof lengthways with a sharp knife but try to keep all the cut leaves together like little bundles of hay.

Place the witlof into a large bowl. Take the walnuts in your hand and crush into irregular pieces over the witlof. Add the snipped chives and the dressing, then carefully roll the leaves around in order to coat them evenly with the dressing but trying to keep them all tidy and together. Place the salad in a tidy mound and finish with some freshly grated parmesan.

Potatoes fried in red wine and coriander seeds

pictured page 146

for six to eight to share

This is a wonderful potato dish that is full of flavour. I find that if I am serving it as a side it works best with goat or lamb, as the wine and spices give the potatoes a good strong flavour.

500 g (1 lb 2 oz) whole, pre-boiled chat or
    nicola potatoes
400 ml (14 fl oz) olive oil
25 g (1 oz/⅓ cup) coriander seeds, toasted and
    ground
2 tablespoons black peppercorns, toasted and
    ground
250 ml (9 fl oz/1 cup) red wine
salt

You will get the best results if you have a saucepan large enough to fit all of the potatoes in a single layer, but it won't matter too much if your pan isn't large enough to accommodate all the potatoes. Take your boiled potatoes and gently press until the skin splits.

Start by heating the oil until nice and hot but not smoking—the best way to test the oil is to place the handle of a wooden spoon into your oil and see if there are any bubbles rising. When the oil is ready, add your potatoes and fry until a golden colour is reached, then carefully turn the potatoes over and fry the other side. Very carefully add your spices and red wine, adding the wine in splashes to start with to avoid the oil boiling over the side of your pan. Keep cooking the potatoes on a high heat until all of the wine has evaporated and the potatoes start to fry once more. The wine will make the potatoes look quite dark but don't panic. When they are ready, gently lift them out of the oil and let them drain on paper towel. Season with salt.

Duck and onion sandwich

for six to eight to share

Sure, this is a sandwich, but it's not just an ordinary sandwich. What I love about it is that it's fancy food played down—the flavours are refined but then the duck is served between 2 slices of bread. It may seem like a lot of effort to go to for a sandwich but the results are superb and it makes a great meal. Try it! The duck is prepared a day in advance, which means that the preparation time on the day is much shorter than it otherwise would be. Also, this gives the duck time to absorb the flavours from the marinade.

1 bunch of thyme
2 cloves of garlic
salt and ground black pepper
4 duck leg quarters with the bone in
4 white onions, cut into large dice
a splash of stock (any type) or water

It is best to start to prepare the duck the day before by taking half of the thyme and 1 of the garlic cloves, chopping them and combining with salt and pepper. Rub this mixture thoroughly over your duck. Cover this and refrigerate overnight.

Preheat your oven to 200°C (400°F/Gas 6). When you are ready to cook the duck, place the duck leg quarters in a roasting tin with the chopped onion, remaining thyme and garlic and stock. Place this into the oven and cook, covered with foil or a lid, for about 2 hours. Remove the foil and cook, uncovered, for a further 20–30 minutes. You will need to stir the mixture together every 20 minutes or so to ensure that everything cooks evenly. While the duck is cooking, start to prepare your onion and pear salad—the baby onions can be baked at the same time as the duck.

For the salad

3 French shallots
salt and ground black pepper
2 tablespoons white wine vinegar
440–650 g (15½ oz–1 lb 7oz/2–3 cups) salt
400 g (14 oz) baby onions, unpeeled
100 ml (3½ fl oz) extra virgin olive oil
a few sprigs of thyme
2 firm but ripe pears such as josephine, corella
   or red danjou
1 punnet baby parsley (you can substitute for
   ½ bunch of flat-leaf/Italian parsley, coarsely
   chopped)

Start by making your dressing. Do this by peeling and very finely slicing the French shallots and mixing well with a good pinch of salt, pepper and vinegar. Let this sit until your onions are ready—this will give the shallot time to pickle slightly.

Preheat your oven to 200°C (400°F/Gas 6), pour a bed of salt onto your roasting tray and stand your onions, root side down, on the salt. This will keep the onions from making contact with the roasting tray and will keep them at an even dry heat. It will take about 25 minutes to cook the onions; to test them for doneness, push a sharp knife into them—they should be very soft all the way through. Leave the oven on.

When they are cool enough to handle, use a sharp knife to cut off the hard root of the onion and remove the skins; if cooked correctly the onions should just about fall out of the skins. Place all the onions in a bowl and drizzle with a little of the extra virgin olive oil and add a few sprigs of thyme and let this sit until you are ready to serve.

To make the salad, cut the pears in half and remove the cores. Using a mandolin or a sharp knife, cut thin slivers of pear and add to the onions along with the parsley. Finish your dressing by whisking the remaining olive oil into the shallot mixture, then pour over your salad and gently fold to combine.

For serving

salt and ground black pepper
1 loaf of Turkish (flat) bread, focaccia or
   schiacciata

Once the duck is tender, remove from the oven but keep the oven on. When cool enough to handle, remove the duck legs and place onto a chopping board. Remove the skin and bone from the duck and place the meat into a large bowl. Using a wooden spoon, mash the meat up until it is well shredded so that there are no pieces of duck, just a smooth mixture of meat. Now add the onions from the duck and mash this mixture together really well, taste for seasoning and if all is good it is ready to stuff your bread with.

Split the bread open lengthways and open up (I find it easier to leave the loaf whole and cut into pieces afterwards). Now spread your duck and onion mix over the bread in a thick layer and close the bread up. The size you cut the sandwiches depends on how you want to serve them. Since I like to get everyone to share everything, I always prefer to cut them into about 4 cm (1½ in) wide strips, which I then put back in the oven for about 10 minutes until hot in the middle and nice and crunchy on the outside. Arrange your sandwiches on a platter and serve the salad over the top.

Bourbon and brownie fool

for four

Even though by strict definition this recipe is not a fool (a fool being a mixture of cream and fruit), it is a pretty accurate way to describe the dish itself and to let you know what you may become if you overindulge in it. I once served these as a canapé at a function and by the end of the night it was easy to tell who the 'bourbon and brownie fools' were.

Because the recipe calls for a good bit of bourbon, you might want to let everyone know this when you serve it—after a belly full of food and wine it might be a little too much for some people.

The good thing about this recipe is that the brownie is great in its own right and will keep in an airtight container for a couple of weeks. In fact, a great way to enjoy this dessert is to bake the brownie and to use the end cuts for the fool and keep the rest for yourself—you only need half the amount for the fool.

If you prefer, you could make this recipe without the rhubarb essence, or use 80 ml (2½ fl oz/⅓ cup) quince syrup from the poached quinces (page 120) instead.

Bourbon and brownie fool
pictured page 152

For the brownies

100 g (3½ oz) unsalted butter, melted
175 g (6 oz/¾ cup) caster (superfine) sugar
2 eggs, lightly beaten
50 g (1¾ oz/heaped ⅓ cup) unsweetened cocoa
    powder, sifted
80 g (2¾ oz/⅔ cup) plain (all-purpose) flour,
    sifted
pinch of salt
175 g (6 oz) Callebaut '811' chocolate callets
    (buttons) or a good-quality dark chocolate
    with around 53% cocoa solids, chopped
165 g (5¾ oz/1⅔ cups) walnuts, toasted
150 g (5½ oz) Callebaut '811' chocolate callets
    (buttons) or a good-quality dark chocolate
    with around 53% cocoa solids, melted
1 teaspoon natural vanilla extract

Preheat the oven to 180°C (350°F/Gas 4). Line an 18 cm (7 in) square baking tin that is about 4 cm (1½ in) deep with baking paper. Mix together the butter and sugar. Combine with the eggs, cocoa powder, flour, salt, chocolate buttons and walnuts, then mix in the melted chocolate and vanilla extract. Pour the batter into the tin and bake for 30 minutes.

For the light rhubarb essence

4 stalks of rhubarb
100 g (3½ oz/½ cup) sugar
a dash of lemon juice

Slice your rhubarb very thinly and sprinkle with the sugar and lemon juice. Combine well in a bowl and leave covered in the fridge for at least 2 hours but preferably overnight. When you are ready to cook the rhubarb, add it to a small saucepan along with a little water to help start the cooking process, making sure that you collect all the juices that form in the bottom of the bowl. Place the rhubarb over a low heat and cook gently for about 25 minutes, or until the rhubarb has cooked to a mush. Pour this into a sieve over a bowl to catch all of the juices, push as much of the juice through as possible and discard the solids.

What you should end up with is a rosy pink, not too sweet rhubarb essence. To intensify the flavours or to make a syrup place this back into your saucepan and cook to the desired result—you should end up with about 60 ml (2 fl oz/¼ cup).

For the fool

half the brownie
300 ml (10½ fl oz) thick (double/heavy) cream
60 g (2¼ oz/heaped ¼ cup) sugar
90 ml (3 fl oz) bourbon
a few leaves of mint

Cut your brownie into small bite-sized pieces and place into a large bowl. Pour over the rhubarb essence, let this sit for a few minutes so the brownie soaks up all of the rhubarb and softens. In a second bowl, whip the cream and sugar together until you have achieved soft peaks. Both these steps can be done in advance and if covered with plastic wrap will sit comfortably in your fridge for a couple of hours. This means it can be done before you sit down to dinner, but the next stage needs to be done as close to serving as possible.

Splash almost all of the bourbon into the chocolate brownie bowl and gently fold just enough to combine. Break the mint into small pieces using your fingers and add to the cream. Using a rubber spatula or your fingers, very gently mix your brownie and cream together until it is only 'just' combined—in fact you get a nicer dessert if it is not properly mixed together. I like to serve this dessert in a glass with a few more pieces of mint scattered over the top. Last of all, splash a tiny bit more bourbon over the top just before it is eaten.

Baba Gewürztraminer
for six

pictured page 153

Typically, a baba is soaked in a syrup made from dark rum. We came up with this version one night when trying to pair a dessert with a particularly delicious Gewürztraminer. I really like the results as this wine variety is big enough in flavour and body to enable some very good flavour combinations. It is best to make the syrup first and allow this to cool while the babas are cooking.

For the syrup

150 ml (5 fl oz) water
335 g (11¾ oz/1½ cups) sugar
6 dried apricots
6 pieces of dried pear
1 vanilla bean, split
400 ml (14 fl oz) Gewürztraminer wine

Start by combining the water and sugar in a saucepan, then place over a high heat and stir until the sugar has dissolved, then add the dried fruit, vanilla bean and wine. Bring back up to heat but do not boil. Just before it is about to simmer, remove from the heat and allow to cool.

For the babas

60 g (2¼ oz/½ cup) raisins
100 ml (3½ fl oz) Gewürztraminer wine
1 teaspoon dried yeast
80 ml (2½ fl oz/⅓ cup) milk, warmed slightly
125 g (4½ oz/1 cup) plain (all-purpose) flour
2 eggs
a big pinch of sugar
a pinch of salt
100 g (3½ oz) unsalted butter, softened

In a small bowl, soak the raisins in the wine and set to one side.

In a large bowl, dissolve the yeast in the milk and let it sit for a moment. Now mix in the flour and eggs and beat until you have a smooth dough, then cover with plastic wrap and allow to prove at room temperature for about 45 minutes.

Preheat your oven to 180°C (350°F/Gas 4). Add the sugar, salt and butter to the batter, mixing vigorously to incorporate. When all of the butter is combined, add the soaked raisins and wine and beat really well again.

Grease a six-hole 125 ml (4 fl oz/½ cup) muffin tin with a little butter before dividing the batter among the holes. Let the mixture rise until the holes are full, then place them in the oven for 20–25 minutes until golden. To test if the babas are ready, insert a skewer and if it comes out clean the babas are cooked.

For serving

When the babas have been allowed to cool slightly, lift them from the tin, place them into the syrup and let them soak for at least 20 minutes. You can actually store the babas in the syrup overnight. When you are ready to serve, lift a baba onto a plate and add a piece of the apricot and pear. Spoon some of the syrup into a saucepan and place onto a high heat and bring to the boil. Pour the hot syrup over the cake and if you feel inclined, serve with a little whipped cream.

Pumpkin pie

for eight to ten

This is a classic recipe. For those of you who think that pumpkin should only be eaten as a savoury food, you have obviously never been enchanted by a well-spiced pumpkin pie! There are a couple of things that you can do with this recipe to personalize it, such as grating a small piece of ginger into your pie filling just before baking or using some maple syrup to replace some of the sugar.

I have given you the quantity of ground spices you'll need. I can't stress enough the difference that you will get if you grind your own spices. It won't be a stronger spice flavour, but it will be more aromatic and pronounced—much more satisfying. The common mistake is that people try to compensate for using pre-ground spices by adding slightly more; I would not recommend doing this as all it really does is make the spice flavour overpowering.

For the pastry

185 g (6½ oz/1½ cups) plain (all-purpose) flour
1 teaspoon salt
120 g (4¼ oz) cold unsalted butter, diced small
4–6 tablespoons ice cold water

Sift the flour and the salt in a bowl, then add the butter and, using a pastry cutter or a fork, cut the butter into the flour until the butter is about half the size of a pea. Start to add a little of the water and use a fork to mix it in; after you have added a couple of tablespoons of water, start using your hands and work until you have a firm, but not hard, dough. Don't add too much water or your dough will be sticky and hard to use, and also the finished pastry will be too tough. Form your dough into a ball and wrap well in plastic wrap and allow to rest for about 2 hours.

Grease a 28 cm (11¼ in) pie tin. Turn your pastry out onto a floured board and, using a rolling pin, roll the pastry until it is about 3 mm (⅛ in) thick. Carefully roll your pastry around your rolling pin to gently lift it onto your pie tin. Gently press the pastry into place with your fingers. Allow this to rest for about 30 minutes in the fridge. Preheat your oven to 180°C (350°F/Gas 4).

Cover the pastry with baking paper, fill with baking beads and blind bake for 15 minutes.

For the filling

3 eggs
185 g (6½ oz/1 cup) soft brown sugar
1 teaspoon ground cinnamon
½ teaspoon ground ginger
¼ teaspoon freshly ground cloves
½ teaspoon salt
500 g (1 lb 2 oz/2 cups) cooked, mashed pumpkin (winter squash) (you'll need to cook about 1.4 kg/3 lb 2 oz pumpkin)
230 ml (7¾ fl oz) pouring (whipping) cream

Preheat your oven to 210°C (415°F/Gas 6–7). In a large bowl, lightly beat your eggs, then add your sugar, spices, salt and mashed pumpkin and mix well. Lastly, add the cream and mix well. Taste your mixture for seasoning and then simply pour into your prepared pie shell and bake in the oven for 40–45 minutes, or until the tip of a knife inserted into the filling comes out clean. Remove from the oven and allow to cool before removing from the pie tin and slicing into pieces. I rarely serve this with anything other than plain whipped cream.

Grown-up hot chocolate and cinnamon donuts

for eight

This is a fun way to finish a meal: beautiful freshly cooked donuts and a nice punchy hot chocolate. Start by preparing the chocolate and then make your donut dough. I like to cook the donuts just before serving as they are infinitely better when served piping hot. What I normally do is set up a tray with the glasses and finish the chocolate while the donuts are cooking, then remove the donuts from the oil, drain them, dunk them straight into the sugar and onto the plate. One word of advice—do not throw away your donut middles! Cook them up—they look great when balanced on top of a stack of donut rings.

For the cinnamon donuts

700 g (1 lb 9 oz/5⅔ cups) plain (all-purpose)
    flour
1 tablespoon baking powder
½ teaspoon salt
¼ teaspoon ground nutmeg
2 teaspoons ground cinnamon
250 g (9 oz/heaped 1 cup) sugar
250 ml (9 fl oz/1 cup) milk
80 g (2¾ oz) butter
1 egg
 vegetable oil, for frying

To make this recipe, you will ideally need a donut cutter—try a kitchenware shop, but you can use a ring cutter instead. Combine the flour, baking powder, salt, nutmeg and half each of the cinnamon and sugar in a large bowl. In a large bowl, combine the milk, butter and egg, then stir into the flour mixture until combined. Cover tightly with plastic wrap, then rest in the fridge for about 30 minutes. Combine the remaining sugar and cinnamon in a large bowl.

Take the bowl out of the fridge and turn out the dough onto a lightly floured surface. Using a lightly floured rolling pin, roll out the dough to just over 1 cm (½ in) in thickness. Using a donut cutter, cut out donuts or you can simply use ring cutters to cut to the size you want (you'll need to cut out a small hole in the middle of each one).

You now need to deep-fry the donuts or you can pan-fry them in a heavy-based frying pan with at least 2 cm (¾ in) of oil. To deep-fry, take a large saucepan and fill it no higher than one-third full of oil. Bring your oil up to 180°C (350°F) and, in batches, carefully lower in your donut rings and middles. Turn twice to ensure even cooking and to make sure they are puffy and golden, 1–2 minutes per side. If you are pan-frying, fry them for 1–2 minutes on each side.

Lift out of the oil, drain on paper towel, then put into a bowl with the remaining sugar and cinnamon and toss about to coat your donuts. Serve as soon as you can.

For the hot chocolate

- 600 ml (21 fl oz) milk
- 400 ml (14 fl oz) cream
- 1 bird's eye chilli
- 1 star anise
- 1 piece of cinnamon
- 2 green cardamom pods, crushed
- a pinch of salt
- 110 g (3¾ oz/scant 1 cup) unsweetened cocoa powder
- 350 g (12 oz) Callebaut '811' chocolate buttons or good-quality dark chocolate, broken into pieces
- 80 g (2¾ oz) bittersweet chocolate, grated
- 185 ml (6 fl oz/¾ cup) crème de cacao
- 30 ml (1 fl oz) Bacardi (white rum)
- 30 ml (1 fl oz) orange juice

Start by combining the milk and cream in a saucepan with your spices and salt. Place this on a very gentle heat and allow to slowly come up to a simmer, stirring from time to time. Allow this mixture to simmer for about another 10 minutes to get as much infused flavour from your spices as possible. Strain.

Place the cocoa into a clean saucepan and add the strained infused milk and cream mixture a little at a time; keep whisking to ensure that there are no lumps. Once all of the milk has been incorporated, add the chocolate buttons and the grated chocolate and whisk well until everything is melted and combined. If you are serving straight away, add the crème de cacao, Bacardi and orange juice and stir well.

If you are not going to serve your hot chocolate straight away, set the mixture aside; alternatively, this can be stored in the fridge and kept for the next day (blended with ice it will make a particularly good chocolate milkshake). When you come to reheat your hot chocolate, place the mixture onto a gentle heat and stir often, without letting the chocolate come to the boil. When you are just about to serve, add the crème de cacao, Bacardi and orange juice and stir thoroughly. Serve with the donuts.

Index

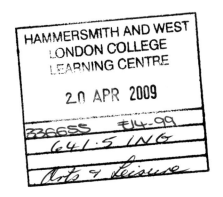
Published by Murdoch Books Pty Limited.
www.murdochbooks.com.au

Murdoch Books Australia
Pier 8/9, 23 Hickson Road, Millers Point NSW 2000
Phone: +61 (0) 2 8220 2000 Fax: +61 (0) 2 8220 2558

Murdoch Books UK Limited
Erico House, 6th Floor North, 93–99 Upper Richmond Road
Putney, London SW15 2TG
Phone: + 44 (0) 20 8785 5995 Fax: + 44 (0) 20 8785 5985

Chief Executive: Juliet Rogers
Publisher: Kay Scarlett

Project manager: Jacqueline Blanchard
Concept and design: Vivien Valk
Production: Adele Troeger
Editor: Zoë Harpham
Photographer: Alan Benson
Stylist: Margot Braddon
Recipe testing: Ross Dobson, Salatiela Cockburn
Drink preparation: Tomas Oleson
Colour reproduction: Splitting Image Colour Studio, Melbourne, Australia

National Library of Australia Cataloguing-in-Publication Data:
Ingersoll, Jared
Sharing plates : a table for all seasons.
Includes index.
ISBN 9781740459631. ISBN 1 74045 963 6.
 1. Cookery. 2. Entertaining. I. Title.641.588

Printed by Midas Printing (Asia) Ltd. PRINTED IN CHINA. First printed 2007.

IMPORTANT: Those who might be at risk from the effects of salmonella poisoning (the elderly, pregnant women, young children and those suffering from immune deficiency diseases) should consult their doctor with any concerns about eating raw eggs.

CONVERSION GUIDE: You may find cooking times vary depending on the oven you are using. For fan-forced ovens, as a general rule, set the oven temperature to 20°C (35°F) lower than indicated in the recipe. We have used 20 ml (4 teaspoon) tablespoon measures. If you are using a 15 ml (3 teaspoon) tablespoon, for most recipes the difference will not be noticeable. However, for recipes using baking powder, gelatine, bicarbonate of soda (baking soda), small amounts of flour and cornflour (cornstarch), add an extra teaspoon for each tablespoon specified.